Nobody Else Like Me

Activities to Celebrate Diversity

by Sally Moomaw

Redleaf Press
St. Paul

"Hello, Hello, Hello" ©1993 2 Spoons Music. Used by permission.
"Nobody Else Like Me" ©1989 2 Spoons Music. Used by permission.
"A Little Like You and a Little Like Me" ©1993 2 Spoons Music. Used by permission.
"I See with My Hands" ©1993 2 Spoons Music. Used by permission.
"Twins" ©1993 2 Spoons Music. Used by permission.
"A Kid Like Me" ©1993 2 Spoons Music. Used by permission.
"May There Always Be Sunshine" ©1964 MCA Music Canada. Used by permission.
"Walkin' on My Wheels" ©1986 Childsong Music, BMI. Used by permission.
"Harry's Glasses" ©1993 2 Spoons Music. Used by permission.
"Everything Possible" ©1993 Pine Barrens Music, BMI. Used by permission.

Published by: Redleaf Press
             a division of Resources for Child Caring
             450 N. Syndicate, Suite 5
             St. Paul, MN 55104

Visit us online at www.redleafpress.org

Library of Congress Cataloging-in-Publication Data

Moomaw, Sally, 1948–
  Nobody else like me : activities to celebrate diversity / by Sally Moomaw.
      p. cm.
Based on the CD by Cathy Fink and Marcy Marxer.
Includes bibliographical references.
  ISBN 1-929610-01-7 (pbk.)
  1. Early childhood education—Activity programs. 2. Ethnicity—Study
and teaching (Early childhood)—Activity programs. I. Title.
  LB1139.35.A37 M66 2002
  372.21—dc21
                                    2002012344

Contents

INTRODUCTION

Welcome to *Nobody Else Like Me*, a collaborative effort between Redleaf Press and musicians Cathy Fink and Marcy Marxer. This is the final book of a series of three that accompany Cathy and Marcy's CDs. The others are *Help Yourself* (2001) and *Changing Channels* (2002). This book was written to help you use the music on this CD to help children and families in your program think critically about and appreciate differences and similarities among people.

How to Use This Book

This book is divided into twelve sections, each of which focuses on one of the songs on the CD. You'll find a brief introduction to each song's developmental content, followed by sheet music and complete lyrics. You can use the sheet music to play the song on a guitar or a piano; many of the songs also work well for singing in circle times without instrumental accompaniment. Or simply sing along with the recording, using the lyrics sheet. We suggest that teachers listen to the whole CD several times and become familiar with the songs before introducing them to the children.

Activities help you explore the topic of each song with children ages three to eight. The first activity for each song gives ideas for using the song itself with children during circle time. The rest of the activities show you how to integrate the topic of the song into your daily curriculum. The activities are designed for a wide age range of children; be sure to evaluate them with your own group in mind, and adapt as necessary to make them work for the children's developmental level.

As more and more children with special needs are included in child care centers and other early childhood programs, it's essential to adapt curriculum to their needs. Many of the activities in this book contain adaptations for children with disabilities (see the Variations).

Cathy and Marcy's music is a great tool for creating curriculum on a variety of topics, and this book will show you how. So open the pages, and turn up the sound!

Nobody Else Like Me (Cambridge, Massachusetts: Rounder Records, 1998) is available as a CD or as a cassette from Redleaf Press, 800-423-8309.

HELLO, HELLO, HELLO

"Hello, Hello, Hello" is a lively greeting song that pulls together three big ideas for children: first, people throughout our communities and around the world greet each other; second, the words they use may sound different yet mean the same thing; and third, children can use greeting words to communicate with children who speak other languages. The song enables teachers and children in primarily English-speaking communities to learn to greet one another in other languages, while teachers and children in bilingual or multilingual communities can expand the song to reflect languages spoken in their schools or neighborhoods. In either case, the song provides a framework for exploring the similarities and differences among the greetings we use.

Hello, Hello, Hello

By Marcy Marxer
©1993 2 Spoons Music, ASCAP

Hello, Hello, Hello

by Marcy Marxer
(©1993 2 Spoons Music, ASCAP)

Hello, hello, hello, (2x)
Boys and girls around the world say
Hello, hello, hello.

Hello, hello, hello, (2x)
Hey, have you heard? What's the word?
It's hello, hello, hello.

Mile after mile, from Hartford to L. A.
A wave and a smile and this is what
we say:

Hello, hello, hello, (2x)
Let's have some fun. You're the one!
Hello, hello, hello.

Hola, hola, (2x)
Boys and girls in Mexico say
Hola, hola.

Hola, hola, (2x)
To say "hello" los niños* say
Hola, hola.

Mile after mile, from Cordoba to
Monterey.
A wave and a smile and this is what
we say:

Hola, hola, (2x)
Let's have some fun. You're the one!
Hola, hola.

Namaste, (2x)
Boys and girls in India say
Namaste.

Namaste, (2x)
To say "hello" the bacha* say
Namaste.

Mile after mile, from Madras to
Bombay.
A wave and a smile and this is what
we say:

Namaste, (2x)
Let's have some fun. You're the one!
Namaste.

Jambo-sana, (2x)
Boys and girls in Africa say
Jambo-sana.

Jambo-sana, (2x)
To say "hello" the watoto* say
Jambo-sana.

Mile after mile, from Nairobi to
Mbale
A wave and a smile and this is what
we say:

Jambo-sana, (2x)
Let's have some fun. You're the one!
Jambo-sana.

Hola! Jambo-sana! Namaste!
Hello, hello, hello!

*los niños, bacha, watoto—all
mean children

WELCOMING ONE ANOTHER

Materials

group-time area, large enough for children to sit comfortably
   together
mat or carpet square for each child to sit on
CD player (optional)

Directions

1. Sing the first verse of "Hello, Hello, Hello" several times with the children so they can become familiar with the words. Use the recording as a backup if it makes you feel more comfortable. On future days, this opening verse can be used to signal the transition to circle time.

2. Add one more verse of the song every few days. This will gradually introduce the children to "hello" in various languages. If you have bilingual or multilingual children in your classroom, start with their home languages. Ask each family to write their word of greeting, if it has a written form, so the children can see the word as they sing it.

3. Repeat the song each day and gradually add greeting words in additional languages.

4. Introduce the American Sign Language sign for *hello* to further support the inclusive theme of this song.

American Sign Language

Discussion

It is important for the children to understand that many, many different languages are spoken in the United States, as well as in other countries. We don't have to go to another country to hear *hola*, *namaste*, and *jambo-sana*. Ask the children questions such as these to help them think about the many languages around them:

- Does anyone you know use a language other than English? Who? What is the language?

- The song says, "Children in Mexico say *'Hola.'*" *Hola* is a word in Spanish. Do you know anyone who speaks Spanish? Where else might you hear children say "Hola" besides Mexico?

Variations

1. During the day, play recordings of songs sung in a variety of languages, such as *The World Sings Goodnight*. This recording includes lullabies sung in thirty-three languages.

2. When you welcome the children to class, occasionally use a greeting word from one of the languages you have been adding to the song.

3. Display a chart with the greeting words in the languages you have included in the "Hello, Hello, Hello" song.

Children's Books

Adler, David A. *A Picture Book of Louis Braille.* New York: Holiday House, 1997. In addition to a captivating story, this book includes a Braille alphabet.

Flodin, Mickey. *Signing for Kids.* New York: Perigee Books, 1991. Signs for many words are illustrated, including "hello."

Raschka, Chris. *Yo! Yes?* New York: Orchard Books, 1993. Using abbreviated language, two boys greet each other and become friends.

Schneider, Jane, and Kathy Kifer. *Braille for the Sighted.* Eugene, Oregon: Garlic Press, 1998. In addition to the Braille alphabet, this book explains how the Braille dots are organized. There are games and activities for practice.

Adult Book

Moomaw, Sally, and Brenda Hieronymus. *More Than Letters.* St. Paul: Redleaf Press, 2001. This activity book shows teachers how to make a big book based on a short poem that includes the words "hello" and "goodbye" in various languages.

Recording

The World Sings Goodnight, 2 volumes. Silver Wave Records, SC 803, SC 909. Description above.

THE RHYTHM OF GREETINGS

Each language has its own unique sound. Focusing on the rhythm of language helps the children become more discriminating listeners and increases their awareness of language patterns. For this activity, the children clap the rhythmic patterns of each of the greeting words used in "Hello, Hello, Hello," as well as greeting words in additional languages introduced into the song in the Welcoming One Another activity. The Rhythm of Greetings activity is excellent for helping the children develop phonemic awareness (the ability to hear the various sounds in words).

Materials

group-time area, large enough for the children to sit comfortably together
mat or carpet square for each child to sit on
CD player (optional)

Directions

1. Sing "Hello, Hello, Hello" with the children.
2. Ask the children to recall the words of greeting they remember from the song.
3. Say each word rhythmically with the children, and then repeat it several times while clapping each syllable. Be sure to emphasize accented syllables.

Discussion

Language is one of the ways we greet people and make them feel welcome. Ask the children for other ways we can make people feel welcome and valued. List their ideas on chart paper and post it in the classroom. Ideas may reflect the varying backgrounds of the children in your class. For example, in some cultures people may smile, while in others they may bow. Pointing may be considered polite in some cultures but rude in others.

Variations

1. After the children have become adept at clapping the sounds of greeting words in various languages, add a rhythm instrument to the activity. Wood blocks or rhythm sticks are easy to play and give one clear sound each time they are struck. The children can play the syllables of the words on the instruments instead of clapping. Children with hearing disabilities or deafness can feel the vibration of the instruments.

2. Continue to add greeting words in various languages to the rhythm activity.

3. Clap other words and play them on instruments. Children particularly enjoy playing the sounds in their names.

Children's Books

Igus, Toyomi. *I See the Rhythm*. San Francisco: Children's Book Press, 1998. This picture book, which won the Coretta Scott King Award, explores the history of African American people through their music: African roots, slave songs, blues, ragtime, jazz, swing, bebop, gospel, rhythm and blues, rock, funk, and rap.

Miranda, Anne. *Let's Get the Rhythm*. New York: Scholastic, 1994. This book encourages movement to a familiar, rhythmical chant.

Pinkney, Brian. *Max Found Two Sticks*. New York: Simon & Schuster, 1994. A young boy explores rhythm and music with "found" instruments from his neighborhood.

Stecher, Miriam B. *Max, the Music Maker*. New York: Lothrop & Lee, 1980. A child plays music on "found" or made-up instruments.

Adult Book

Moomaw, Sally. *More Than Singing*. St. Paul: Redleaf Press, 1997. Chapter 3 introduces rhythmic patterns, including the words for "friend" in various languages, for the children to clap and play on instruments.

Flags Galore

The international flavor of "Hello, Hello, Hello" suggests coordinating it with the visual symbols of flags. You can share storybooks that have flag illustrations with the children to give them some grounding in the association of flags with people of particular cultures. You can also make a memory game for the children using flags as the symbols to match. Young children have difficulty understanding concepts such as city, state, and country, so naturally the idea of flags and what they represent is too abstract for them to easily comprehend. Nevertheless, they are intrigued with the colors, shapes, and forms they see on flags and may begin to associate them with the people they know in class or see in the community.

Materials

children's books that include flag illustrations, such as *What Is Your Language?*, by Debra Leventhal

index cards, 3 by 5 inches

flag illustrations, which can be copied from books or downloaded from Internet sites, to mount on the cards (You will need two copies of each flag.)

Directions

1. Read a book that includes flag illustrations to the class, and include it in the book area. *What Is Your Language?* is a good choice because the repeating text, which can also be sung, introduces the children to the words "yes" and "no" in languages from many parts of the world. Prominent in the illustrations are the flags representative of those countries.

2. Design a flag memory game for the children to use in the classroom. Two copies of each flag in *What Is Your Language?*, or flag drawings copied from Internet sites or reference books, can be mounted on index cards and laminated.

3. The children can spread the cards face down on the floor and take turns finding matches. Be sure to include the flags of any international children in the class. The children may enjoy saying "hello," "yes," or "no" in the language of the culture represented by the flags they select.

Discussion

Use questions such as these to help extend the children's mathematical thinking as they play with the flags:

- How many flags do you have so far? If you get two more flags, how many will you have?
- How many of your flags have stripes (or stars, or some other color or pattern)?
- Both the U.S. flag and the flag of Great Britain have red, white, and blue colors. How can you tell the flags apart?

Variations

1. Start the game with about ten sets of matches so that the children are not overwhelmed by the number of cards. Gradually add flags to expand the children's observational skills as well as to add complexity and interest to the game.

2. Display flags in the classroom. Small flags mounted on flagpoles are readily available or can be made.

3. Ask the children to discuss with their families where their ancestors came from. Help them locate the flags for those countries through reference materials.

Children's Books

Leventhal, Debra. *What Is Your Language?* New York: Dutton, 1994. Description above.

Students of the G. T. Cunningham Elementary School. *We Are All Related: A Celebration of Our Cultural Heritage.* Vancouver: Polestar Book Publishers, 1996. In this remarkable book, the children explore their cultures and roots through both drawings and words. Many children include symbols from their cultures.

"Hello" Language Center

Children are fascinated with the way words look and sound in various languages. The word "hello," translated into the languages most prevalent in the classroom, community, or region, can be incorporated into a classroom writing center.

Materials
index cards or sentence strips (lined tagboard)
dark-color marker
sandpaper
lightweight paper
pencils

Directions
1. Carefully write the word for *hello* in several languages on index cards or sentence strips and place them in a basket on a writing table or shelf. Matching letters or symbols, such as Chinese or Hebrew characters, can be printed or drawn on index cards and cut to a size that fits over the letters or symbols on the *hello* word cards. The children can match the letters and symbols to the corresponding words.

2. Cut letters or symbols for the word *hello,* or its equivalent in various languages, from sandpaper and glue them onto tagboard. The children, including those with visual disabilities, can trace the letters or characters with their fingers or create rubbings by placing lightweight paper over the sandpaper symbols and rubbing across them with the sides of crayons.

3. The children can use the word cards for *hello* in various languages as models to help them write the words. Children at diverse stages of writing, from scribbling to making recognizable symbols, may enjoy this activity. Some children find it very interesting to copy the symbols used in writing from a culture other than their own.

Discussion
Most countries and communities include people who speak several different languages. To help young children understand this, relate

this discussion to the classroom, school, or community, so that they can draw connections to real people they have met. For example, you might say:

> "People speak lots of languages in our town. Mr. Gonzalez, who teaches fifth grade upstairs, can speak Spanish and English. Mrs. Kim, who owns the store we visited, speaks Korean and English. Next week, when we visit the Native American Cultural Center, maybe Mr. Irwin will teach us how to say 'hello' in Lakota, his language. Should we ask him?"

Variations

1. Add "Hello" blank books to the language area. These books can be easily made by cutting sheets of construction paper into thirds to create 4- by 9-inch strips. These strips can be folded in half to form the front and back covers of each book. Cut inexpensive paper into similar strips and fold to form the inside pages. Staple the pages together to create the blank books. The children may enjoy writing the various *hello* words in these books.
2. Add word cards for *goodbye* in various languages to the language center.

Children's Books

Feelings, Muriel. *Jambo Means Hello.* New York: Dial Books, 1974. This alphabet book uses Swahili words to represent the letters. The black and white illustrations, which locate the words in their central or eastern African context, earned illustrator Tom Feelings a Caldecott Honor book award.

Lee, Huy Voun. *In the Snow.* New York: Henry Holt and Company, 1995. A mother draws Chinese characters in the snow as she explains to her child how the symbols are related to pictures.

Scott, Ann Herbert. *Hi!* New York: Philomel Books, 1994. A young child repeatedly tries to say "hi" to people but is ignored until a postal worker responds to her.

Kye Kye Kule

Children love participating in the movements of "Kye Kye Kule," a traditional call and response song from Ghana. Many children are already familiar with movement songs, either from home, child care settings, or school. They may have sung songs such as "Where Is Thumbkin" from the time they were tots. Introducing "Kye Kye Kule" to the class, with its familiar movements and catchy rhythms, shows the children that action songs are part of many cultures. They can compare the directions in "Kye Kye Kule" with songs they already know and see the similarities.

Songs such as "Kye Kye Kule" are rooted in culture. Presenting the song along with a children's book, written by an author from Ghana or someone who is very familiar with the country, places the song within the context of a particular culture. The children can then relate the song to a group of people (in this case Ashanti), their environment, and their culture. It is also helpful to compare the song to other songs that the children are familiar with. For example, many children sing the following song:

Heads, shoulders, knees and toes, knees and toes,
Heads, shoulders, knees and toes, knees and toes,
Eyes and ears and mouth and nose,
Heads, shoulders, knees and toes, knees and toes

It is very similar to "Kye Kye Kule." Many traditional African American songs also have a call-and-response pattern and include movements, no doubt reflecting their African roots. By singing songs from various cultures that have similar content, you can help the children understand the similarities among peoples.

Kye Kye Kule

Kye Kye Ku - le *(chay chay koo - lay)* Kye Kye Ko - fi Sa *(chay chay koh - fee sah)*

Ko - fi Sa Lan - ga *(koh - fee sah lahn - gah)* Ka - ka Shi - lan - ga *(kah - kah shee lahn - gah)*

Kum A - den Nde *(koom ah - dehn day)* Kum A - den Nde Hey!

Traditional (Ghana)
arrangement by Cathy Fink & Marcy Marxer
2 Spoons Music, ASCAP

Kye Kye Kule

Traditional (Ghana)
arrangement by Cathy Fink & Marcy Marxer
(2 Spoons Music, ASCAP)

Kye Kye Kule
(chay chay koo-lay)

Kye Kye Kofi Sa
(chay chay koh-fee sah)

Kofi Sa Langa
(koh-fee sah lahn-gah)

Kaka Shilanga
(kah-kah shee lahn-gah)

Kum Aden Nde
(koom ah-dehn day)

Kum Aden Nde Hey!

Hands on your head
Hands on your shoulders
Hands on your waist
Hands on your knees
Hands on your ankles
Hands on your ankles hey!

PLAY KYE KYE KULE

Materials

group-time area, large enough for the children to move without
  bumping into each other
CD player
children's book set in Ghana, such as *Anansi Finds a Fool*
  (see Children's Books list)

Directions

1. Assemble the children in the group-time area, perhaps with a transition song, such as "May There Always Be Sunshine," sung with the children's names (see page 102).
2. Have the children stand. Ask them to make sure they have room to move their arms without bumping anyone.
3. Play the recording of "Kye Kye Kule." Encourage the children to join in as you act out the movements to the song.
4. Follow this active song with a quieter activity, such as reading a story from Ghana.

Discussion

Use questions such as the following to help the children relate "Kye Kye Kule" to movement songs with which they are already familiar:

- Is "Kye Kye Kule" like any other movement songs you know? Which ones? How are they alike? How are they different?
- Is it easier to do what the song says when it's slower or when it's faster? Which speed do you like the best? Why?

Variations

1. After the children have become familiar with "Kye Kye Kule," introduce other action songs. The book and recording "Shake It to the One That You Love the Best," referenced below, includes traditional African American songs.
2. The children will notice the tempo increase in "Kye Kye Kule" as the song progresses. This is one of the factors that make the song

so much fun. During the day, play other music with a tempo increase, called "accelerando" in musical terminology. A notable example, and one that many children enjoy, is "In the Hall of the Mountain King" from Edvard Grieg's *Peer Gynt*.

Children's Books

Aardema, Verna. *Anansi Finds a Fool.* New York: Dial Books, 1992. In this Ashanti tale, Anansi wants to have all the riches but do none of the work. He is tricked by his friend to teach him a lesson.

Mattox, Cheryl W. (ed.) *Shake It to the One That You Love the Best: Play Songs and Lullabies from Black Musical Traditions.* Nashville: JTG, 1991. This collection of traditional African American songs has stunning illustrations to share with the children.

Recordings

Marley-Booker, Cedella, with Taj Mahal. *Smilin' Island of Song.* Warner Brothers, 42521. This delightful Jamaican reggae recording is very appealing to young children.

Shake It to the One That You Love the Best. Music for Little People, MLP 2211. This recording features traditional African American songs and complements the book listed above.

Video

Fink, Cathy, and Marcy Marxer. *Is Not, Is Too.* Community Music, 1996. This video shows Cathy and Marcy performing "Kye Kye Kule" live with an audience, so you can see the activity in motion.

STORIES FROM GHANA

Singing a song from a culture that is not your own can seem strange and exotic unless it is put into an appropriate context. While the children enjoy the rhythms and movements of "Kye Kye Kule," they can understand and appreciate the song much better when they know something about the people and culture it originates from. "Kye Kye Kule" is a song of the Ashanti people of what is now Ghana, in West Africa. Several children's books introduce children to the Ashanti people through traditional stories with beautiful illustrations. *Anansi Finds a Fool* is one. Written by Verna Aardema, it tells the story of the lazy Anansi, who is tricked by his friend. Children from preschool through primary grades enjoy this captivating story.

Materials

group-time area, large enough for the children to sit comfortably together, or cozy reading area for reading to several children at a time

copy of *Anansi Finds a Fool*, available in libraries, bookstores, and through Internet booksellers

additional books about Ghana or the Ashanti people

Directions

1. After the children have become familiar with "Kye Kye Kule," introduce them to *Anansi Finds a Fool*.
2. Read the book during group time, or place it in the book area for small-group book sharing.
3. Primary-age children may also enjoy Verna Aardema's book *Misoso*, which includes twelve tales from Africa, of which two are Ashanti.

Discussion

Anansi Finds a Fool provides plenty of material for discussion. Use questions such as these to encourage children to think about the issues of laziness, greed, and trickery raised by the story:

- How did you feel about Anansi wanting to get all the fish without doing any of the work? (To connect this to their own lives, ask how

they would feel if they baked a batch of cookies, and then their brother and his friends ate them all?)
- Do you sometimes do things for other people without expecting a reward? How does that feel? (For example, we may feel very good inside after helping rake the leaves for an elderly neighbor.)
- Was it all right for Bonsu to trick Anansi because he was teaching him a lesson? When is it okay to trick people, and when is it not okay?

Variations

1. Introduce additional books about the Ashanti people and Ghana. The children may enjoy reading some of the other books by Verna Aardema, such as *Why Mosquitoes Buzz in People's Ears.*

2. Many cultures have so-called teaching tales that deal with issues similar to *Anansi Finds a Fool.* For example, the Diné (Navajo) trickster story *Ma'ii and Cousin Horned Toad,* by Shonto Begay, describes a tricky coyote that loves to eat but hates to work. Does this sound familiar? The children can compare the coyote to Anansi and discuss their similarities.

Children's Books

Aardema, Verna. *Why Mosquitoes Buzz in People's Ears.* New York: Dial Books, 1990. In this West African tale, Mosquito's story causes a disaster in the jungle. The illustrations are spectacular.

Aardema, Verna. *Misoso: Once upon a Time Tales from Africa.* New York: Alfred A. Knopf, 1994. Described above.

Begay, Shonto. *Ma'ii and Cousin Horned Toad.* New York: Scholastic, 1992. Described above.

Littlefield, Holly. *Colors of Ghana.* Minneapolis: Carolrhoda Books, 1999. The children can learn about the people, traditions, land, and resources of Ghana through this exploration of colors.

Musgrove, Margaret. *The Spider Weaver: A Legend of Kente Cloth.* New York: Scholastic, 2001. Two Ashanti weavers learn the secret of weaving kente cloth by watching a spider. This traditional cloth from Ghana is widely admired. The illustrations are vibrant.

African Music

"Kye Kye Kule" introduces the children to a song from Africa, accompanied by a catchy rhythm played on a drum. Much of the music of Africa is very rhythmical; as a matter of fact, rhythmic patterns are often layered one on top of another to produce a complex rhythmic texture. By having the opportunity to listen to recordings of African music, the children can gain a better feel for the variety and complexity of the music. Recordings of African music can be found in many libraries and are also available in the international sections of many music- and bookstores.

Materials

cozy listening area, perhaps with cushions or small rocking chairs
CD player or tape recorder
recordings of African music (Many good recordings of African music are available through the Smithsonian Folkways label. Their Web address is www.folkways.si.edu.)
photographs of African musicians (optional, but desirable)

Directions

1. Set up a cozy area in the classroom where the children can listen to music during the day.
2. Introduce the recordings of African music.
3. Be prepared to scaffold or support the children as they listen to music that may not sound familiar to them. If the children comment that they don't like the music, acknowledge their feelings and then direct their attention to some interesting aspect of the music, such as the drums.
4. Leave the recordings out for several weeks. It takes both children and adults time to become familiar and comfortable with music that is new to them.

Discussion

To some children, music from Africa sounds very different from what they are accustomed to. There is often much less emphasis on melody, so they may not hear tunes that they can sing. On the other hand, the complex rhythms may at first sound overwhelming. By building on aspects of the music that are similar to things the children are familiar with, you can help them gradually begin to appreciate a style of music that is new to them. Many children soon begin to request the African music recordings during choice time. Use questions and comments such as these to help the children discuss their reactions to the music:

- This music sounds different to you, and you're not sure you like it. Robbie, I remember how much you like playing the drums when we get them out. Let's listen to the drums in this piece. Those drummers are playing really fast.
- Oh, listen. I hear a flute. I really like flutes, and I want to hear how this one sounds.

Variations

1. Start with one recording of African music and gradually add more. Many recordings feature music from several African countries or cultures. As they become more skilled listeners, the children may begin to distinguish various types of African music.

2. Some children may want to "play along" as they listen to the music. Add some of the African instruments discussed in the following activity, Playing African Instruments, to the area for the children to explore. This is especially important for children with hearing disabilities as it gives them the opportunity to participate.

Recordings

Africa: Drum, Chant, and Instrumental Music. Nonesuch, 9–72073–2. This recording features music from Niger, Mali, and Upper Volta.

Balafons and African Drums, 2 volumes. PlayaSound, PS 65101, PS 65156. The groups Koko and Sababougnouma, from Burkina Faso, perform exciting, rhythmically complex music on *balafons* (African xylophones) and assorted drums from the culture. Koko's balafon player also sings.

Playing African Instruments

Playing music is exciting for young children. The children can gain a much better appreciation for African music if they can experiment with playing some of the instruments used in the recordings. Various types of African instruments are available in early childhood catalogs, music catalogs, and African stores and Web sites. Some of the most appropriate and interesting instruments for young children are tongue or slit drums, which are hollow wooden boxes with "tongues" of different lengths cut into the top to produce various pitches; *shekeres*, from West Africa, which are hollow gourds with a netting of beans stretched over the outside to produce a rattling sound; and West African gourd rattles, which have slices of dried gourd mounted on a stick for shaking.

Materials

small music area in the classroom, with a low bench or table to hold several instruments
several African instruments, such as those described above
recording of African music (optional)

Directions

1. Start with one type of instrument in the music area. The tongue drums are very exciting and make a good first instrument.
2. If possible, include two drums in the area, reducing the wait time for this exciting activity and allowing the children to play together.
3. After the drums have been available for several days, consider playing a recording of African music in the music area. Many children like to play along with the recording.
4. After the children have had a week or more to experiment with the tongue drums, add a second type of African instrument, perhaps gourd rattles.
5. After another week or so, add a third instrument, such as the shekeres. At this point you may decide to put the tongue drums away for a time so the children can focus on the sounds of the shaken instruments.

Discussion

Once the children have experimented with various types of African instruments, they may be much more astute listeners. Use questions such as these to help children describe their experiences with the instruments used in class:

- Which drum makes the loudest sound? Why do you think that is?
- Does the way you strike the drum change the sound? How? How can you tell?
- What instruments do you have in your home? What instruments have you heard at parties, or at church (or other locations with which you know the children are familiar)?
- How are the African instruments the same as those instruments? How are they different?

Variations

1. Once the children have had plenty of time to experiment with the African instruments, develop a listening game. Hiding the instruments behind a screen, play each instrument and let the children try to determine what it is.
2. Make your own tongue drums. Details for making tongue drums can be found in *More Than Singing* (see below).
3. Some cities have African music or dance ensembles. Arrange a field trip to attend a rehearsal or concert, or members of the group may be willing to visit the classroom.

Children's Book

Pinkney, Andrea, and Brian Pinkney. *Shake Shake Shake*. San Diego: Harcourt Brace, 1997. This rhythmical text shows children playing with a shekere.

Adult Book

Moomaw, Sally. *More Than Singing*. St. Paul: Redleaf Press, 1997. Activity 5.8 shows how to make a tongue drum. Other African and multicultural instruments are also featured in this book.

NOBODY ELSE LIKE ME

3

Teachers of young children understand how important it is to help all children develop positive individual and group identities. As children struggle to discover how they fit into their family, neighborhood, community, and the broader world, teachers can plan activities that help them answer questions such as "Who am I?" and "What is special about me?" Listening to and singing the words to the song "Nobody Else Like Me" can help weave together some of the many answers to this question. The names of the children in the class can be easily substituted into the song so that every child feels special.

Nobody Else Like Me

By Marcy Marxer
©1989 2 Spoons Music, ASCAP

Nobody Else Like Me

by Marcy Marxer

(©1989 2 Spoons Music, ASCAP)

There's nobody else like me,
I'm as happy as I can be
From my head to my toes, yeah, everyone knows
There's nobody quite like me

There's nobody else like me,
As the world can plainly see,
From the place I reside
To the stories inside,
There's nobody else like me,

bridge:
I can sing a song,
(la-da-da-da-da-da) or play along
Or whistle, or yodel-o-dle-ay-dee-tee,

I love to joke and play,
I'm learning new things every day,
From tying my shoes to the things in the news,
There's nobody else like me.

bridge

There's nobody else like me,
I'm as happy as I can be
From my head to my toes, hey, everyone knows
There's nobody else like me,
Yeah!

Singing about You and Me

Materials

group-time area, large enough for the children to sit comfortably
  together
mat or carpet square for each child to sit on
CD player (optional)

Directions

1. Sing the first verse of the song several times with the children so
   they can become familiar with the words. Use the recording as a
   backup if it makes you feel more comfortable.

2. Substitute the name of a child into the song to replace the words
   "me" and "I." Naturally the pronouns will also need to be altered.

   > There's nobody else like *Juanito*,
   > He's as happy as he can be
   > From his head to his toes, yeah
   > Everyone knows
   > There's nobody else like *Juanito*.

3. Continue around the circle until every child has had a chance to
   hear their name in the song.

Discussion

"Nobody Else Like Me" celebrates the happy feelings we all have at
certain times. Naturally, we also experience times when we are not
happy. Use these questions to help the children develop a rich
vocabulary of "feelings words" and discuss the variety of ways they
can feel.

- Ask the children to think of times when they felt sad, angry, scared,
  or unwelcome. Consider adding more complex words such as *dis-
  appointed*, *frustrated*, and *jealous*. What made them feel that way?
  What did they do with their feelings? Did they tell someone? Did
  anything help to make them feel better?

- Ask the children to think of times when they noticed other people
  feeling sad, angry, scared, or unwelcome. What did they do? What
  do they think might have helped the other person? What do they
  want from other people when they are upset?

Variations

1. "Nobody Else Like Me" can serve as a welcoming song and help the children make the transition into the group setting. After each verse, the child highlighted might tell one thing that's special about herself. List these special traits or interests on chart paper next to each child's name.

2. Children experience many different feelings. Before each child's verse, ask how the child is feeling right now, and that emotion can be added to the song in place of "happy." For example:

> There's nobody else like *Yao*,
> She's as *sleepy* as she can be . . .

3. Children love adding movements to songs. Try singing the song standing up. The children can reach to their heads and toes as they sing those words of the song. Then other body parts can be substituted, based on suggestions from the children. For example:

> There's nobody else like *Beth*,
> She's as happy as she can be,
> From her *shoulders* to her *knees*,
> Everyone knows,
> There's nobody else like *Beth*.

4. Throughout the day, spontaneously sing "Nobody Else Like Me" and acknowledge children's activities and feelings. The song can help comfort children who are sad, reassure those who are anxious, and welcome new children into the class. These are just of few of the ways the song can be woven into the life of the classroom.

Children's Books

Mayer, Mercer. *You're the Scaredy-Cat.* Columbus, Ohio: McGraw Hill, 1974. Two boys camp out in the backyard. The one telling scary stories ends up scaring himself.

Simon, Norma. *I Was So Mad!* Morton Grove, Illinois: Albert Whitman & Company, 1974. A young girl acknowledges the things that make her mad. The book gives children permission to voice this emotion.

Nobody Else Like Keesha—Classroom Diaries

Classroom diaries, which are a joint contribution of parents, children, and teachers, are a wonderful way to celebrate the uniqueness of each child. Photographs, drawings, documentation of activities, writing and art samples, and notes and recollections from parents are all wonderful ways to share and record the ways in which each child is special. The diaries can be kept in the classroom to be read and shared by the children throughout the year.

Materials

notebook or folder for each child

preprinted pages to be filled out by the parent, such as family background and favorite activities of their child

special note to the children from their families documenting why they are so special to them

photographs of the children, both at home and at school

special artwork, writing, or story dictation selected by each child for inclusion

Directions

1. Introduce the idea of the diary to the parents before the start of school or close to the beginning of the year, perhaps on a home visit or during open house.

2. Design a cover for each child's diary. This could be a photograph or a self-portrait drawn by the child.

3. Send home special pages of the diary to be filled out by the parents.

4. Throughout the year, add photographs of the children and examples of their work to their diaries.

5. Read the diaries with the children frequently, and encourage them to share their diaries with other children.

Discussion

The children can begin to explore diversity by first getting to know themselves better. Use questions such as those on the following page to help the children think about what's important about them.

- What makes you really happy? What makes you sad, or angry?
- What's your favorite thing to do with your family?
- What's scary?
- What do you like to do outside?

Variations

1. Many children like to share their diaries with the group. Arrange for the children to "read" their diaries to the class during group time, with perhaps one child per day or several children per week.

2. Children with visual disabilities can have their diary pages written in Braille or enlarged print, whichever is appropriate.

3. Ask for help from language specialists to sign the key words in diaries of children who are deaf and learning sign language.

Children's Books

Cheltenham Elementary School Kindergartners. *We Are All Alike . . . We Are All Different.* New York: Scholastic, 1991. In this book, the children describe why they are all alike, but also ways in which they all differ. This multicultural book is illustrated with the children's artwork and color photographs.

Lacapa, Kathleen, and Michael Lacapa. *Less Than Half, More Than Whole.* Taylor, Arizona: Storytellers Publishing House, 2001. A young Native American boy wonders about his identity when a friend tells him he's not all Indian, maybe only half. His grandfather helps him understand the uniqueness of each person.

Rogers, Fred. *Let's Talk About It: Extraordinary Friends.* New York: Puffin Books, 2000. With beautiful photographs and clear text, Mr. Rogers introduces six children with disabilities and explains that although all children are special, they share many similar feelings.

Watch Us Grow, and Grow, and Grow . . .

Children are naturally excited to hear from adults about how fast they are growing. When spring comes and last year's clothes don't fit, they have real documentation. Taking height and weight measurements throughout the year and charting each child's growth is a way to involve the children with measurement and help them understand the growing process. The intent of the activity is to help the children celebrate their own growth journeys rather than to compare sizes with one another.

Materials

photographs of the children throughout the year, perhaps standing next to the same object in the classroom, so they have a basis of comparison
chart paper for each child, to record the child's height
simple bar graph for each child, to indicate weight changes
baby photos and clothes for each child, sent to school by the parents

Directions

1. Photograph each child at the beginning of the year and several times throughout the year so they can see how they are growing and changing. If the cost of film is an issue, ask the parents or community resources for donations. Some stores may develop the film for free as a donation.

2. Measure the height of each child, perhaps with a piece of yarn that stretches the length of the child and is glued or stapled to chart paper. The relationship between a child's height and a length of string or yarn may be easier for young children to understand than marks on paper to indicate the tops of their heads.

3. Create a simple bar graph for each child, showing the changes in their weight. The children can compare the columns at various times during the year.

4. Ask the parents to send baby photos and baby clothes to school. The children can compare how they looked as babies with how they look now. They can also compare the size of the clothing to their bodies now and see how much they have grown.

Discussion

It's easy for children to fall into the habit of comparing their heights with one another. In our society, there is a strong preference for being tall, especially among men. It's important for the children to realize that we all have our own growth rates, and whether we are tall, short, or somewhere in between does not matter. Help the children come to these realizations by asking questions such as these:

- What's good about being tall? What's good about being short?
- Is there anything frustrating about being tall? Is there anything short people are better at?

Variations

1. Instead of measuring the children with string, trace around their bodies at the beginning of the year. Later, trace around each child again in a different-color marker, perhaps on top of the first tracing. The children can compare how the sizes of all of their body parts have changed.

2. Help the children compare the growth in their hands and feet. The children can dip their hands and feet in paint and press them onto paper. Later in the year, they can repeat the activity and compare the size of their hands and feet.

Children's Books

Hutchins, Pat. *Happy Birthday, Sam.* New York: Greenwillow Books, 1978. On his birthday, Sam discovers that he still can't reach many of the things he needs. However, by standing on a small chair that is a birthday gift from his grandparents, he is able to reach everything he wants.

Hutchins, Pat. *You'll Soon Grow into Them, Titch.* New York: Greenwillow Books, 1983. Titch keeps getting hand-me-down clothes from his older siblings who have outgrown them. When a baby arrives, Titch can finally hand down some clothes of his own.

Marzollo, Jean. *How Kids Grow.* New York: Scholastic, 1998. This multicultural book shows children at different ages and emphasizes their growing skills.

Raffi. *Everything Grows.* New York: Crown Publishers, 1989. This book, which can be sung, emphasizes that everything alive grows, including children.

SELF-PORTRAITS

Drawing, painting, and sculpting with clay are some of the many ways children express themselves. Creating self-portraits can be a source of pleasure and insight for the children. With the help of photographs, mirrors, and appropriate art materials, the children can study their faces and work to replicate their unique face maps.

Materials

photograph of each child's face
several small mirrors on stands, such as cosmetic mirrors
crayons, pencils, or markers, in multicultural skin, eye, and
  hair tones
drawing paper

Directions

1. Set up an activity table so that several children can work at the same time.
2. Decide ahead of time what art media you will use—crayons, pencils, or markers. Keep in mind that while markers are easy to use, they cannot be used to create shading.
3. Place a mirror in front of each workstation. The children can examine their faces as they draw.
4. Provide a photograph of each child's face for comparison.
5. Support the children's endeavors through questions and comments. For example, help the children match shades of art materials to their skin and hair. They can also point out the shape of faces and eyes, where the eyebrows are located, and how the mouth looks. These comments are to help the children's observations, not to judge their artwork.

Discussion

Children in all classrooms will naturally be at various stages in their art development. Support the children at each stage and value the process of creating. To encourage the children to talk about their work, use comments and questions such as these:

- Tell me about your drawing.
- Oh, that's the head. Yup, heads sure are round, just like that.
- You drew green hair. Wow, it's so bright!

Variations

1. The children can use a variety of art media to express themselves. Try the same activity throughout the year using a variety of materials. For example, paint in multicultural skin tones can be substituted for drawing materials.

2. Children are readily drawn to clay because of its tactile properties. It is an ideal medium for children with visual disabilities or blindness because they can feel their creations as they emerge. After they have had experience working and experimenting with clay, the children can begin to create busts of themselves. Mirrors and photographs, along with your support, can help the children in their endeavors.

3. Plan a parent night so that the families can share in their children's school experiences. The families can work together with paint or clay, perhaps to create family portraits or busts.

Children's Books

Ancona, George. *Earth Daughter*. New York: Simon & Schuster, 1995. Ancona uses brilliant color photographs to help relate how a young girl from Ácoma Pueblo learns the traditional art of pottery making.

Hoffman, Eric. *Best Best Colors*. St. Paul: Redleaf Press, 1999. A young boy and his friends talk about their favorite things—including colors. With his two mothers, he decides to use all the colors to create a flag for a pride parade.

Hucko, Bruce. *A Rainbow at Night: The World in Words and Pictures by Navajo Children*. San Francisco: Chronicle Books, 1996. In this stunning book, Navajo children describe themselves and their culture through their artwork.

SPECIAL KIDS

4

Sometimes teachers comment that there is no diversity in their classrooms. What they usually mean is that all of the children are from the same race. In actuality, all classrooms are diverse because all children and families are unique. While the children may share the same racial background, they may come from families of different religious or socioeconomic backgrounds. All families have historic and cultural roots that affect their outlook on children and family life. The uniqueness of families and children will fill any classroom with diversity.

One of the big tasks for the children is discovering who they are, where they come from, and what kinds of people they hope to be. Through the words of real children, beautifully accompanied by the hammered dulcimer, "Special Kids" conveys what is important to the children as they examine themselves. Some children describe family backgrounds and countries of origin, while others talk about personality traits, talents, and what they like. Through class books such as those created in We Are Special—Class Books, the children can relate what is special about them. Every child can participate at his or her level, regardless of abilities. The strong message of "Special Kids" is that we are all unique. Everyone is special.

A "Special Kids" note from Cathy and Marcy

The "Special Kids" recording on *Nobody Else Like Me* was a spontaneous afterthought that turned into a wonderful learning experience for all involved. The University Park Elementary School Ensemble had just completed their part of the recording, singing on choruses and refrains to the songs. They had done a wonderful job. As we were thanking them, and looking over the diversity in the room, just for fun we had each student say into a microphone something they felt was special about themselves. The answers were beautiful—talking about their heritages, cultures, favorite sports, and personality traits.

At the same time, we noticed how the whole group listened and learned each time a different student talked about what was special about themselves. They were discovering something new about their friends and paying deep attention to each other. Their choral director was delighted and also learned from the experience.

After the students left, Marcy and I realized we had a real gem on tape. A little editing would tie together the words, directly out of the children's mouths, into a story that was part of what defined that group of people. We decided to add a backdrop of gentle hammered dulcimer music lending beauty, but not distraction.

Many variations of this activity are possible. Some schools have an audio-visual department with tape recorders and other recording equipment. Many parents and family members have recording know-how and equipment on their computers. A local recording studio may even donate a little time to facilitate an experience like this. Teachers might also combine the auditory experience with a visual one by adding pictures of students to accompany the recorded words. The tape with the book of photos could be made available in the classroom listening center. If recording equipment is not available, the children's words can be transcribed and combined with photos to make a book for the class library. Just the experience of saying what makes you special, and listening as your friends do the same, can be powerful for children. Older students may even participate in choosing background music, from classical to folk to jazz and more.

More variations for older students

1. Have students interview each other, in a group setting. One student asks questions of another, who speaks into a microphone (or not). Instead of the one sentence "sound bites" on "Special Kids," perhaps there will be four to five questions giving the whole class a chance to learn more about each student. Take turns with interviewers and interviewees, so that everyone has a turn. Meantime, other students are becoming good listeners and learning about one another. This activity can be spread out over several days or weeks.

2. Have students serve as the interviewer for parents, grandparents, siblings, and others at home. They can bring the recorded results to class (see if a hand-held tape machine from the school might be signed out). These interviews can then be shared with classmates or used in the listening center with books made about the interviewees by the students.

WE ARE SPECIAL—CLASS BOOK

Materials

photograph of each child in the class
white drawing paper
pencils
colored pencils
two pieces of colored construction paper

Directions

1. Mount a photograph of each child to the top of a piece of drawing paper.

2. Listen to the song "Special Kids" with a small group of children.

3. After talking about the song, encourage the children to write about what is special or important to them. Children who are too young to write can dictate their responses.

4. Give the children colored pencils to draw about themselves and the important people in their lives.

5. Use the colored construction paper for the front and back covers of the book. Print "We Are Special" on the front of the book for the title.

6. Staple or bind all of the pages together to create a class book.

7. Read the book at circle time, or encourage the children to read their individual pages.

8. Display the book in the classroom so the children can refer to it frequently.

Discussion

Use questions such as the following to help the children focus on the important things about them:

- Who is in your family? What's special about your family?
- What is your favorite thing to do with your family?
- Who are your friends? What do you like about them?
- What do you like best to do at school or child care?

Variations

1. The pages from the "We Are Special" book make excellent remembrances for the children and their families. When you are finished using the book in the classroom, it can be disassembled. Each child's page can be sent home or placed in a special scrapbook of school memories.

2. Children love looking at photographs of themselves and their friends. Repeat the activity several times during the year using photographs of the children engaged in different activities.

3. Compile each child's series of pages into an "I Am Special" book. Each child will have a book by the end of the year.

Children's Books

Cheltenham Elementary School Kindergartners. *We Are All Alike . . . We Are All Different*. New York: Scholastic, 1991. This multicultural book is illustrated with the children's artwork and color photographs. The children describe why they are all alike, but also ways in which they all differ.

Hucko, Bruce. *A Rainbow at Night: The World in Words and Pictures by Navajo Children*. San Francisco: Chronicle Books, 1996. In this stunning book, Navajo children describe themselves and their culture through their artwork.

Students of the G.T. Cunningham Elementary School. *We Are All Related: A Celebration of Our Cultural Heritage*. Vancouver: Polestar Book Publishers, 1996. In this impressive book, children explore their cultures and roots through both drawings and words. Each child's story and artwork are unique.

LIKES AND DISLIKES

All of us have things that we like and things that we don't like. Sharing our ideas with others sometimes causes us to rethink our positions. For example, in a kindergarten class one child said she hated alligators, while another child said he really liked them. After listening to his reasons, the first child revised her opinion and decided she liked alligators as long as they were in zoos. In this activity, the children have the opportunity to express what they like and dislike and have their feelings listened to.

Materials

children's books that discuss what the character likes and dislikes, such as those listed below

chart paper, divided into three columns, with the children's names listed in the left column, their likes in the center column, and their dislikes in the right column

Directions

1. Read one of the books listed below, or a similar book of your choice, to a small group of children to spur discussion about the things they like or don't like.

2. Ask the children, one at a time, to tell you something they especially like and something they don't like. Young children sometimes have trouble responding to a negative question, so they may not be able to give an answer for something they don't like. It's fine to leave the column blank. Avoid putting children's names in either the positive or negative columns. The purpose of the activity is not to compare the popularity of the children (see Discussion).

3. Carefully print the children's responses in the appropriate columns.

4. Allow the children plenty of time to discuss their responses with you and with one another.

5. Post the chart in the classroom for the children to refer to.

Discussion

Teachers should always plan ahead for the possibility that sensitive topics may emerge. For example, what would you do if a child said they didn't like another child? While this might be an honest response, it would also be very hurtful and would need to be dealt with appropriately. In almost every case, there would be some specific behavior that the child didn't like, so you might say, "Does Patty do something that bothers you?" If the child replies, "She hits me," you could acknowledge that hitting hurts and suggest ways for helping Patty learn not to hit, such as helping her talk. Follow up with a positive statement, such as "I really like the way Patty runs up and hugs me when she gets to school. It makes me feel so good." This helps the children realize that all of us have positive and negative traits.

Variations

1. The children may wish to compile their reflections about what they like and don't like into individual books. They can write or dictate a comment at the top of each page and then illustrate it below. The pages can be stapled into a book.

2. The children's ideas can also be compiled into a class book. Each child can have a page in the book that describes the likes and dislikes of each.

Children's Books

Eyvindson, Peter. *Kyle's Bath*. Winnipeg: Pemmican Publications, 1984. Kyle has many things that he likes, but his bath is not one of them.

Johnson, Angela. *The Girl Who Wore Snakes*. New York: Orchard Books, 1993. Many people dislike snakes. Not Ali! This young African American girl discovers that she loves snakes.

Wood, Audrey. *King Bidgood's in the Bathtub*. New York: Harcourt, 1986. In contrast to Kyle, King Bidgood loves his bath, and many other things as well.

FAMILY CELEBRATION—
CLASS QUILTS

Family celebrations are a wonderful way to celebrate the special aspects of each child and family in the classroom. Families are often eager to come to school when they know they will be sharing in a class project with their child and understand that their contributions are valued. The class quilt project allows families to contribute a square to the quilt that celebrates their own culture, heritage, or family. The squares are then mounted together to form a group quilt. The quilt metaphor embraces two issues of fundamental importance: we are all unique, but we also share a commonality. Each family has a part of the quilt that expresses their individuality, but all of the squares form a shared class endeavor—a real coming together of all parties.

Quilts or special types of fabric are part of the cultures of most societies. Looking at quilts and fabrics provides an opportunity for the children to observe and discuss the unique aspects of various cultures as well as their similarities. For example, while a traditional quilt from Hawaii looks very different from an Amish quilt, both are warm and soft and express the artistry of the people who made them. Many children have a special blanket, perhaps crocheted or sewn by their grandma, auntie, mom, or dad, that they would like to share with the class. The children can be encouraged to describe what is special to them about their quilt or blanket.

Materials
white felt, cut into 12- by 12-inch squares
permanent markers, in assorted colors
glue
assortment of buttons, spangles, beads, and paper or felt cutouts
needles and thread

Directions
1. Before the celebration, send a letter to each family explaining the class quilt. Encourage the families to bring any items from home that they would like to add to the quilt, such as fabric from their culture or special trinkets.

2. Divide the classroom into workstations so that the families can work together. Provide at least one felt square for each family and

plenty of art materials.

3. Encourage the families to represent things that are important to them on their quilt square.

4. Label each family's quilt square.

5. After the squares have dried, sew them together to form a group quilt or mount them to a felt backing with spray adhesive (for the non-sewers!).

6. Display the quilt in the classroom or school.

Variations

1. The children may enjoy making other types of class quilts. Provide squares of white cotton fabric for the children to draw on with fabric markers. The squares can then be sewn together to create a class story quilt.

2. The children can also sew on colorful burlap to create a class quilt. Burlap in bright colors is available at some fabric stores. Cut a square of burlap for each child and mount it in an embroidery hoop for support during the sewing process. The children can use large plastic needles, colorful yarn, and large beads to create designs on their quilt squares. These can then be combined into a class quilt.

Children's Books

Gilman, Phoebe. *Something from Nothing*. New York: Scholastic, 1992. In this captivating story, a young boy's special blanket is transformed by his grandfather into something special each time it wears out.

Guback, Georgia. *Luka's Quilt*. New York: Greenwillow Books, 1994. A grandmother makes her granddaughter a traditional Hawaiian quilt, but the child doesn't like it at first because it uses only two colors.

Jonas, Ann. *The Quilt*. New York: Greenwillow Books, 1984. A young girl's parents make her a special quilt out of fabric from clothes she has outgrown. That night, she dreams an adventure derived from scenes on the quilt.

Adult Book

Moomaw, Sally, and Brenda Hieronymus. *More Than Painting*. St. Paul: Redleaf Press, 1999. Chapter 6 includes ideas for making a variety of types of quilts with children.

Dulcimer Music

The song "Special Kids" features children talking about themselves over a lovely accompaniment played on the hammered dulcimer. The hammered dulcimer figures prominently in American folk music as well as in music from many parts of the Near East and Europe. Listening to music played on the hammered dulcimer exposes the children to music they may not be familiar with and widens their musical horizons. Hammered dulcimer music provides a calming backdrop for other classroom activities, such as painting and drawing.

Materials

CD player
recordings of hammered dulcimer music
paint or drawing implements

Directions

1. Play the song "Special Kids" for a small group of children. Draw attention to the musical background in the song and ask the children to describe how the hammered dulcimer sounds to them.

2. Distribute the art materials you have selected. Tempera paint, watercolors, crayons, colored pencils, and markers are all possibilities.

3. Play a recording of hammered dulcimer music while the children express themselves with art materials. Encourage the children to listen to the music as they create and express the feelings the music evokes with their art materials.

4. Add a stringed instrument, such as a child's zither or Autoharp, to the music area of the classroom. Children who are Deaf or have difficulty hearing the recording of the dulcimer can feel the vibrations of the strings as they experiment with the instrument.

Discussion

Sometimes teachers feel that the only music children will listen to are recordings of children's songs. Actually, children are fascinated by many types of music. One way to provide a more multicultural curriculum is to include diverse music drawn from a variety of cultures. The children can listen for the similarities and differences among various types of music. In the process, their listening skills develop and their musical tastes broaden. Many children and adults find the music of the hammered dulcimer pleasant and easy to listen to. This makes it an excellent choice to include in early childhood classrooms.

Variations

1. Nothing can top a live performance to pique the children's interest and help them understand the nature of music. Ask at your local music store or look on the Web (www.rtpnet.org/~hdweb) for a musician to visit your class and play the hammered dulcimer. It need not be a professional musician. Many adults play the hammered dulcimer for relaxation and recreation.

2. Provide recordings of a variety of types of music for the children to listen to during choice time. Jazz, classical music, ethnic music, and international music provide a wide selection.

Children's Books

Curtis, Gavin. *The Bat Boy and His Violin.* New York: Simon & Schuster, 1998. A father, who coaches a team in the Negro baseball league, learns to appreciate his young son's violin playing.

Isadora, Rachel. *Ben's Trumpet.* New York: Greenwillow Books, 1979. A young boy longs to play the trumpet just like the musicians at the clubs. Then a trumpet player takes him in hand.

Moss, Lloyd. *Zin! Zin! Zin! A Violin.* New York: Scholastic, 1995. With a rhythmic, rhyming text, this Caldecott honor book introduces the instruments of the orchestra.

Recordings

There are many great hammered dulcimer recordings available. Look for recordings by Malcolm Dalglish, John McCutcheon, Maggie Sansone, Evan Carawan, or the group Trapezoid. Elderly Instruments (www.elderly.com) is a great source for these recordings.

A Little Like You and a Little Like Me

5

"A Little Like You and a Little Like Me" celebrates the uniqueness of each individual as well as our commonality as people. This is the essence of multicultural curriculum: calling attention to our rich diversity while we acknowledge our sameness as human beings.

The song "A Little Like You and a Little Like Me" refers to skin colors as red, brown, black, and white. It's important for children to recognize that these words don't reflect the reality of people's skin tones. In discussions during activities, comment that while people sometimes refer to skin tones as red, black, or white, all of us have skin in shades of brown or tan. Children who refer to themselves as white can compare their skin color to the white of the paper used for the body tracings in the first activity, for example.

A Little Like You and a Little Like Me

By Cathy Fink
©1993 2 Spoons Music, ASCAP

A Little Like You and a Little Like Me

by Cathy Fink

(©1993 2 Spoons Music, ASCAP)

Every child born into this world
Is a little like you and a little like me,
We all cry and eat and giggle and gurgle,
A little like you and a little like me.
Brown skin, black, yellow, red and white,
A little like you and a little like me,
We see the sun by day, the moon by
     night,
A little like you and a little like me.

chorus:
Everybody's just a little bit different,
From how we look to saying our names,
Everybody's just a little bit different,
And we can celebrate the ways we're not
     the same.

Some kids eat curry and some eat rice
A little like you and a little like me,
Some eat noodles with garlic and spice,
A little like you and a little like me.
Some kids eat meat, others never do,
A little like you and a little like me,
We eat with chopsticks, forks, and
     fingers too,
A little like you and a little like me.

chorus

We've got dreadlocks, goldilocks, lox
     and bagels
A little like you and a little like me,
We've got beads, barrettes, braids,
     and bangles,
A little like you and a little like me.
Brown hair, blond hair, red hair,
     blue hair,
A little like you and a little like me,
Wild hair, tame hair, gray hair, no hair,
A little like you and a little like me.

chorus

Some of our friends like to dance
     the polka,
A little like you and a little like me,
In my neighborhood we like to rock
     and roll-a,
A little like you and a little like me.
I've seen people rap and dance like
     Hammer,
A little like you and a little like me,
Just get with the music and dance
     together,
A little like you and a little like me.

Our Bodies—The Same, Yet Different

Exploring their bodies through body tracings is one way for the children to focus on what is the same and different about each of them.

Materials

large roll of white paper, 36 inches wide
multicultural markers representing a variety of skin tones
tempera paint representing a variety of skin tones
tempera paint in assorted colors
variety of sizes of paintbrushes
CD player

Directions

1. Ask the children to take turns lying on their backs on 5-foot lengths of white paper while an adult, or in the case of older children, another child, traces around their bodies. Describe the body part you are currently outlining to enhance vocabulary and language development. Have each child help select a skin-tone marker that closely matches their skin color.

2. Once several body tracings are completed, ask the children to compare what is the same and what is different about their body tracings.

3. Next, the children can fill in their body outlines with the color of paint that best matches their skin tones.

4. As the children paint, play the recording of "A Little Like You and a Little Like Me." This will provide a pleasant backdrop for the activity and refocus the children's attention on what is the same and different about their bodies.

5. While the paint from the first group dries, begin the tracing and painting process with another small group.

6. When the paint has completely dried, the children can add detail to their bodies, such as features, clothing, and hair.

7. Once the body tracings are displayed in the classroom or hallway, lead the children on a gallery tour. Documenting the children's responses as they create their body images and take their gallery

walk can give insights for further areas to explore as children discover what is the same and different about their bodies. Selected books, such as those listed below, can help the children answer their questions.

Discussion

Comments and questions such as the following can help the children examine what is the same and what is different about them and their classmates:

- What have you noticed about Maria's skin color?
- Is it similar to Takuo's? To someone else's?
- Look at the way LaKeisha painted her hair to look curly.
- David's hair looks very straight and long.
- What color did you use to paint your toenails, Lela?
- We all have toenails, don't we, and some children's are hidden in their shoes!

Variations

1. Plan activities such as painting the outlines of hands and feet at other times, especially when you want to revisit the concepts of *same* and *different.*

2. A variety of collage material can be offered for children who want to add yarn for hair or fabric for clothing to their body tracings.

3. For children who are blind or have visual disabilities, trace the body outlines with puffy paint. Once the paint is dry, help the children feel the various parts of their body tracings.

Children's Books

Ewald, Wendy. *The Best Part of Me.* Boston: Little, Brown & Company, 2002. Children talk about their bodies in pictures and words in this delightful book.

Kirk, Daniel. *Bigger.* New York: G. P. Putnam's Sons, 1998. With simple text, a child explains how he has grown and developed.

Marzollo, Jean. *How Kids Grow.* New York: Scholastic, 1998. This book highlights multicultural children at different ages and stages of development.

HAIR MATCHING GAME

One of the topics covered in the song "A Little Like You and a Little Like Me" is hair variation, including color, texture, and style. This matching game encourages the children to look closely at their hair and compare colors and textures.

Materials

hair samples, provided by family, friends, or hairstylists
white poster board
glue
clear Con-Tact Paper or lamination film

Directions

1. Collect a wide variety of hair samples. Be sure to include hair in various colors and textures, from tightly curled to straight.

2. Cut the white poster board into 4-inch squares.

3. Glue a small clump of hair onto each square of poster board. Be sure to include two squares with each hair sample so the children can match them.

4. Cover the cards with Con-Tact Paper or lamination film.

5. Place the cards in a small basket on the manipulative or science shelf. The children can match the hair samples or group them by various attributes, such as putting all the curly hair together.

Discussion

As the children match and group the hair samples, talk with them about characteristics of their own hair, the hair of their family members, and the hair of other children in the class. Below are some examples of possible comments or questions to interject into the discussion:

- Tell me about your hair, Hanna.
- Is your hair the same color as your brother Ben's hair?
- Why do you think people in the same family sometimes have hair that looks or feels the same?

- How is your hair similar or different from the hair of your friends Amit and Wei?
- Does everybody have hair?

Variations

1. With younger children, start with fewer samples of hair and add more examples later as they become familiar with matching them.

2. Older children may not feel challenged with just matching the hair samples. They may prefer to use the cards to play a memory game. The cards can be placed face down and turned over two at a time as children attempt to make matches.

3. Children with visual disabilities should have hair samples that are not covered with Con-Tact Paper. In this way, they feel the hair texture. Be sure the hair samples are sanitized, perhaps by rubbing them with alcohol.

4. Older children may become interested in talking about what animals are mammals and therefore have hair.

Children's Books

Cheltenham Elementary School Kindergartners. *We Are All Alike . . . We Are All Different.* New York: Scholastic, 1991. The children describe ways in which they are alike and different, including their hair. This multicultural book is illustrated with the children's artwork and color photographs.

Burnie, David. *Mammals.* New York: Dorling Kindersley, 1993. This fascinating book groups mammals by various categories, including mammals on the move, furry friends, careful parents, animals playing, and many others.

Kroll, Virginia L. *Hats Off to Hair.* Watertown, Massachusetts: Charlesbridge Publishing, 1995. Variations of hair and hairstyles from around the world are colorfully depicted.

Nikola-Lisa, W. *Bein' with You This Way.* New York: Lee & Low, 1994. Issues of same and different are skillfully handled through a delightfully rhythmic text.

ALL ABOUT ME

"A Little Like You and a Little Like Me" explores many ways in which people are the same and different, including physical attributes and emotions. This literacy activity encourages the children to describe themselves, both inside and out, building on the contrasting descriptions of feelings in Audrey Wood's book *I'm as Quick as a Cricket*.

Materials

copy of the book *I'm as Quick as a Cricket*
story paper (blank on the top and lined on the bottom)
colored pencils or markers
CD player

Directions

1. During group time, listen to the song "A Little Like You and a Little Like Me." The children can join in on the repeating refrain as they become familiar with the words.

2. Read the book *I'm as Quick as a Cricket* to the class. After the story, give each child a chance to describe how he or she feels.

3. At a later time, introduce the writing part of the activity to the children in small groups. Refer to the Audrey Wood book and reread some of the pages. Let the children discuss how they feel.

4. Assist the children in writing descriptions of their feelings. Younger children can dictate their ideas. Since *I'm as Quick as a Cricket* employs the simile construction "I'm as . . ." throughout, many children will use this in their descriptions of themselves.

5. Encourage the children to illustrate their ideas in the blank area of the paper.

Discussion

All of us experience a wide range of emotions, and we feel differently about ourselves at different times. This range of feelings that makes up who we are is beautifully described in *I'm as Quick as a Cricket*; however, young children may not comprehend this unless some discussion is facilitated. Use questions and comments such as the following to help children identify the feelings in the story:

- The child in the story says he is "as small as an ant." Ask the children if they ever feel little. If they say "no," comment, "I feel little when I'm in the car and a lot of trucks go by. Sometimes I feel as little as a bug next to those trucks." This may encourage the children to think about times when they also feel little.

- The child in the story also says he is "as large as a whale." Again, ask the children if they ever feel huge like a whale. If they say "no," make a comment such as, "I feel big when I'm looking at an anthill. The ants are so tiny, sometimes I feel like a skyscraper next to them."

Variations

1. Children often want to share their stories with the class. They can help you read them during group time. The children should be given the option of whether or not they wish to share their descriptions of themselves.

2. The children's individual stories can be combined into a class book to place in the book area.

3. You may wish to create story starters to help children generate ideas and serve as print models. Print samples using the simile construction from the book, such as:

> I'm as playful as a puppy.
> I'm as big as a dinosaur.
> I'm as bouncy as a ball.

Use stickers to illustrate the story starters for any children who are not yet readers.

4. To extend the activity, add the story paper, story starters, and a copy of the book to the class writing center. The children can continue writing their feelings and descriptions whenever they are interested.

Children's Books

Bang, Molly. *When Sophie Gets Angry—Really, Really Angry . . . .* New York: The Blue Sky Press, 1999. Sophie learns how to relax in a natural setting to get over her angry feelings.

Clifton, Lucille. *Everett Anderson's Goodbye.* New York: Henry Holt and Company, 1983. Everett has to deal with his many emotions after the loss of his father.

Viorst, Judith. *Alexander and the Terrible, Horrible, No Good, Very Bad Day.* New York: Atheneum, 1972. Alexander has one of those days when everything goes wrong. He learns that some days are like that.

Wood, Audrey. *I'm as Quick as a Cricket.* Singapore: Child's Play Ltd., 1990. Described above.

OUR FAMILIES

Talking about families provides an important way for children to appreciate similarities among people while becoming comfortable with differences. Family photographs can stimulate the children to think about their roots and what is important to them about their family, and to share their families with other children. Noted Cree artist George Littlechild incorporates photographs of his family and ancestors into his paintings. In his book *This Land Is My Land*, he describes what various family members have meant to him through words and artwork. This book can serve as a catalyst for the children to begin exploring their own family ties through photographs, writing, artwork, and conversations with family members.

This provides an excellent opportunity for the children to become aware of the variety in family organization. For example, a child may live with her mother and father, a single parent, grandparents, an extended family, a blended family, two mommies or daddies, or rotate between two family units. She may have many brothers and sisters or be the only child in the family. Some children have families that regularly come to school, perhaps during drop-off and pick-up times; others may ride a bus to school, so their families seldom visit. In one classroom, a child shared his family drawing with another child and said, "I see your mommy every day. Now you can see mine."

Materials

copy of the book *This Land Is My Land*
photocopies of family pictures for each child
white drawing paper
markers or colored pencils

Directions

1. Send home a letter to parents asking them to send a family photo to class, or take family photographs during home visits. Make several photocopies of each child's family photograph.

2. Read a few selected pages from *This Land Is My Land* to the class. Discuss how Littlechild has incorporated photographs of his family into his artwork.

3. Each child can glue the photocopy of their family photo onto drawing paper and incorporate it into a picture of what is

important to them about their families.

4. After the children have completed their artwork, they can write or dictate their thoughts about their families. Their family reflections can be displayed with their artwork. Children may wish to take turns reading their reflections to the class and talking about their families.

Discussion

Help the children think about the variety in their families by asking questions and making comments such as the following:

- Who are the people in your family picture?
- Kyle lives with his dad, and Leticia lives with her mom.
- Cindy and Nhung both have baby sisters.

Variations

1. Using the George Littlechild book as a model, children at the G. T. Cunningham Elementary School in Vancouver engaged in an extensive cultural heritage project. They incorporated photographs of their families into their artwork and wrote about family ties. Their work has been published in a beautiful book, *We Are All Related*. The children can use this book as a resource as they work on their own family projects. Many cultures and ethnicities are represented.

2. Incorporate a similar family heritage project during a family night at school. The families can work together embedding their family photographs into a family drawing or painting.

Children's Books

Brynjolson, Rhian. *Foster Baby*. Winnipeg: Pemmican Publications, 1996. A Native American baby is lovingly cared for by his Native foster family.

Hoffman, Eric. *Best Best Colors*. St. Paul: Redleaf Press, 1999. Nate has several special friends and two loving mamas.

Littlechild, George. *This Land Is My Land*. San Francisco: Children's Book Press, 1993. Described above.

Rylant, Cynthia. *When I Was Young in the Mountains*. New York: Dutton Children's Books, 1982. This lyrical book may spur the children's interests about how their grandparents lived.

Students of the G. T. Cunningham Elementary School. *We Are All Related: A Celebration of Our Cultural Heritage*. Vancouver: Polestar Book Publishers, 1996. Described above.

I See with My Hands

6

"I See with My Hands" emphasizes the use of touch to compensate for blindness. The song is not strictly accurate; many of the things named in it cannot be touched by blind people ("the clouds, the sky, the land . . ."), and most blind people would not refer to themselves as seeing with their hands. However, the song offers the opportunity to discuss the sense of touch with the children, and opens the door to activities that will deepen the children's understanding of what it means to be blind and the ways in which people who are blind or visually impaired navigate the world and perform everyday tasks.

While the song does a good job of emphasizing the abilities of people with visual impairments, the children also need to recognize that blindness poses severe challenges, especially in an environment that is not designed for non-sighted people. Children with normal vision rely on visual input. They may not realize the many obstacles that individuals with visual disabilities or blindness face. While it is true that individuals with visual disabilities rely strongly on other senses, including touch, there are some things they cannot "see" or perceive by touching. Discuss with the children what some of these things might be. Examples could include clouds, stars, mountains, and sunsets.

I See with My Hands

I see with my hands, The clouds, the sky, the land, The
I see with my hands, The clouds, the sky, the land, A
I see with my hands, The clouds, the sky, the land, A

fish that swim in the deep blue sea, The sun that shines on you and me,
bird, a flower, a warm em-brace, And my best friend's smil-ing face,
stone, a stream, a mel-o-dy, The peo-ple in my fam-i-ly,

I see with my hands.   hands.   hands.
I see with my
I see with my

BRIDGE
See,_____ see,_____ eve-ry cu-ri-o-si-ty,_____

See,_____ see,_____ in my hands I hold the key;_____

By Marcy Marxer
©1993 2 Spoons Music, ASCAP

I See with My Hands

by Marcy Marxer

(©1993 2 Spoons Music, ASCAP)

I see with my hands,
The clouds, the sky, the land,
The fish that swim in the deep blue sea,
The sun that shines on you and me,
I see with my hands.

I see with my hands,
The clouds, the sky, the land,
A bird, a flower, a warm embrace,
And my best friend's smiling face,
I see with my hands.

bridge:
See, see, every curiosity,
See, see, in my hands I hold the key;

I see with my hands,
The clouds, the sky, the land,
A stone, a stream, a melody,
The people in my family,
I see with my hands.

bridge

I see with my hands,
The clouds, the sky, the land,
The fish that swim in the deep blue sea,
The sun that shines on you and me,
I see with my hands.

SEEING THINGS MY WAY

A good complement to the song is the delightful book *Seeing Things My Way,* by Alden R. Carter, which uses color photography and first-person narrative to describe how a young, visually impaired girl and her blind or visually impaired friends use a variety of tools, many of which rely on touch, to help them. While all of us use our sense of touch hundreds of times a day, we may not be aware of how much information we can gain by touching things. This activity gives the children a chance to match and identify objects without relying on sight.

Materials
copy of the book *Seeing Things My Way*
feely box (Cut the bottom off a sock, stretch it over the top of a
  small box, and tape it in place.)
pairs of small items to place in the box, such as combs, toy cars,
  twigs, pinecones, sponges, and plastic animals
CD player

Directions
1. Listen to "I See with My Hands" with the children. Encourage them to talk about things they like to touch and things that are unsafe to touch.

2. Place the feely box on a manipulative shelf, science table, or special activity table. Put one object from each pair inside the box, and the other object on a tray or in a basket next to the feely box. The children can take turns feeling the objects, making matches, and identifying the items by touch.

3. Read the book *Seeing Things My Way* with the class.

Discussion
Use questions such as these to deepen the children's understanding of the issues raised in the song:

• What things named in the song could you experience by feeling them?

- What things in the song could you not experience by touch?
- What things in our school could a blind person use or experience by feeling them? What things could they not use by feeling them?

Variations

1. Add different items to the box every day or two to provide additional challenges and stimulate interest.

2. "I See with My Hands" talks about "seeing" a friend's smiling face by touching it. Working in pairs, the children can attempt to identify facial expressions by touch. It's not easy! After washing their hands, children can sit across from one another and take turns closing their eyes and feeling the face of the child across from them. They can try to determine if the child is smiling, frowning, or showing some other emotion. The children may prefer to have a scarf tied over their eyes to make it easier to keep them shut. Be sure each child agrees to the use of the blindfold. Never blindfold a child who is not comfortable with it.

Children's Books

Adler, David A. *A Picture Book of Louis Braille.* New York: Holiday House, 1997. This book describes how Louis Braille, accidentally blinded as a child, grows up to invent the Braille alphabet.

Carter, Alden R. *Seeing Things My Way.* Morton Grove, Illinois: Albert Whitman & Company, 1998. Described above.

BRAILLE—WHAT IS IT?

Many individuals who are blind or have severely impaired vision learn to read Braille, a system of writing in which raised dots in various patterns are used to represent letters. If you have a child in your classroom who is blind, you may already be labeling environmental print with Braille and have Braille books in the classroom. Whether any children in the class have visual disabilities or not, the children will benefit from being exposed to Braille and learning what it is. They may have already noticed Braille in elevators or on signs. Having Braille books in the classroom, or adding Braille to books you already have, gives the children a chance to explore a new way of writing and speculate about what it is like to learn to read by feel.

Materials

copy of *A Picture Book of Louis Braille*, by David A. Adler
several children's books written in Braille
duplicate books written in standard print
several classroom signs with their Braille equivalent added to them

Directions

1. Show the children *A Picture Book of Louis Braille.* The book is written in standard print with lovely color illustrations. Each page has a clear plastic overlay with the words written in Braille.

2. Read a familiar children's book to the class. Then show them the same book written in Braille. Public libraries, special education resource centers, the Association for the Blind, and the National Braille Press (listed below), all have Braille books.

3. Display the books together in the classroom. Encourage the children to feel the Braille and look for any patterns they can find in the writing.

4. If there is an elevator or sign with Braille labels in your school or in a building nearby, take the children in small groups to see and feel it. Talk about how important it is for blind people to have signs that they can read.

Discussion

- If a blind person came to our school, what materials would be easy for them to use? What materials would be hard or impossible for them to use?
- How could someone who couldn't see find their way around our school? Are there things we could change to make that easier?

Variations

1. *A Picture Book of Louis Braille* tells the story of Louis Braille and how he invented the Braille system of writing for the blind. His story is one of tremendous courage and insight. Primary-age children will enjoy hearing the book read to them. Shorten the text for preschool and kindergarten children or tell the story in words familiar to them.

2. Investigate having a class visitor read a book to the children that is written in Braille. They may have many questions, such as what it was like to learn to read in Braille. The Association for the Blind may be able to help.

3. Some children may become quite curious about what the alphabet letters look like in Braille. Add a Braille alphabet to the class writing center. Braille alphabets can be downloaded from the Web site of the National Braille Press, and embossed copies can be ordered from them free of charge. *A Picture Book of Louis Braille* has a Braille alphabet juxtaposed over a printed alphabet in the back.

Children's Books

Adler, David A. *A Picture Book of Louis Braille.* New York: Holiday House, 1997. Described above.

Schneider, Jane, and Kathy Kifer. *Braille for the Sighted.* Eugene, Oregon: Garlic Press, 1998. This book describes how the Braille alphabet is organized. Primary children may wish to try some of the Braille games and activities.

Web site

National Braille Press: www.nbp.org. This Web site lists helpful resources for parents or teachers, including how to order a free Braille alphabet.

Can You Tell by Listening?

Children with normal vision are accustomed to relying on their eyes. They forget how much information comes from hearing. This activity gives them the opportunity to focus on listening skills.

Materials

group-time area, large enough for the children to sit comfortably together

four different rhythm instruments, such as a tone block, triangle, maraca, and jingle bells

box, flannelboard, or some other type of screen behind which to hide the instruments

Directions

1. Show the instruments to the children, and play them one at a time. Let the children discuss how each instrument sounds.

2. Play the instruments, one at a time, behind the screen. Let the children determine by listening which instrument you are playing.

3. After playing each instrument, hold it up so the children can compare the sound to the appearance of the instrument.

4. If you have a child with a hearing disability in the class, plan ahead for how they can participate. Perhaps they can visually identify the instruments as they are held up. After the group activity, they can have the opportunity to play the instruments and feel the vibrations.

5. Vary the number of instruments you use depending on the age and needs of the children. If four instruments are too many, start with just two or three and add more later.

Discussion

Ask the children to think about all the things they listen to during the day. You can list their responses on chart paper. Then have the children close their eyes and listen for several minutes (as long as they can sit quietly). Have the children describe the various things they heard.

Variations

1. Expand listening activities by creating a tape recording of environmental sounds. A telephone ringing, water running in the sink, a car door slamming, a dog barking, and a car engine starting are just a few of the possibilities. The children can listen to the tape and identify the sounds. You can also play a lotto game by making game boards from photos of the items that make the sounds (a telephone, the faucet, a dog, a car, and so on). When the tape is played, the children put markers on the pictures that match the sounds.

2. Tapes of animal sounds are available in stores or catalogs. They can be placed in a listening area of the classroom along with picture books of the animals on the tape.

3. *Polar Bear, Polar Bear, What Do You Hear?*, by Bill Martin Jr., focuses on the sounds of animals. Once the children are familiar with the book, they can create their own listening book. Working with individual children or small groups, you can have the children close their eyes and listen. The children can replace the words "polar bear" in the repeating text with their own names and list what they hear.

> *Nancy, Nancy*, what do you hear?
> I hear *LaToya* whispering in my ear.

Children's Books

Isadora, Rachel. *Bring on That Beat*. New York: Putnam, 2002. With its simple, rhythmic text, this book describes the sights and sounds of Harlem in 1938. It is an urban celebration.

Martin, Bill Jr. *Polar Bear, Polar Bear, What Do You Hear?* New York: Henry Holt and Company, 1991. Described above.

Recordings

53 All-American Bird Songs and Calls. Special Music Company, SMC–4592. Children are fascinated with the variety of birdcalls on this recording. Some they may recognize, and others are new.

A Walk in the Forest. Special Music Company, SMC–4989. This soothing recording includes forest sounds, such as a bubbling stream, a bullfrog, a woodpecker, and wind blowing through the trees.

WHAT DO YOU SMELL?

Smelling is perhaps the most underutilized sense for many of us. While most of us are aware that many of our animal cousins have a much better sense of smell than we do, there are many things that we can identify by smell. The noted physicist Richard Feynman once experimented with developing his sense of smell and found that he could learn to tell by scent which book out of a group had recently been held by a person. This activity helps the children focus on their sense of smell.

Materials

area of the classroom large enough for you to sit comfortably with several children, such as a special activity table

variety of items with strong odors, such as a rose, an orange, an onion, a banana, coffee, peppermint, and cedar

Directions

1. Have the children close their eyes or pull a loose scarf or blindfold over their own eyes.
2. One at a time, bring out the items for smelling. Hold each item close to the children so they can sniff it. Give the children time to discuss and describe what they think they are smelling.
3. After each item has been presented, have the children open their eyes or raise their blindfolds to see the object.
4. Repeat the process with each item.

Discussion

Use questions such as the following to help the children think about why our sense of smell is important.

- Has anyone ever been somewhere that smelled wonderful? Where was it? What smelled so good?
- Can you think of something dangerous that our sense of smell could warn us about?

Variations

1. The children may enjoy reading about animals and their highly developed sense of smell. Several suggestions are listed below.

2. Expand on the smelling activity by putting smelling jars into the science area. The jars have a slit cut in the top so that the children can sniff them. Film containers are a convenient size to use. The lids are easy to cut and can be glued onto the jars after the material for sniffing is placed inside.

3. Arrange for a field trip to a flower conservatory or garden. The children can take a sniffing tour and enjoy the beauty of the various scents.

Children's Books

Bare, Colleen Stanley. *Sammy, Dog Detective*. New York: Scholastic, 1998. This highly trained police dog uses many senses, including smell, to assist police investigations.

Bemelmans, Ludwig. *Madeleine's Rescue*. New York: Puffin Books, 1978. Madeleine is rescued by a small dog in this delightful story.

Hickman, Pamela. *Animal Senses: How Animals See, Hear, Taste, Smell, and Feel*. Toronto: Kids Can Press, 1998. The children learn how animals use all of their senses, including smell, in this informative book.

The song "Twins" is about twins who switch clothes so they can fool their teacher. Being a twin can be a source of both joy and frustration. Twins often delight in each other as playmates, sticking together against all odds. At the same time, like all children, twins need to be seen as individuals and to develop their own identities. Despite their bond, twins usually have all the issues common to siblings. Their twin-ness is often the first thing strangers comment on, and even people they know well may have difficulty seeing beyond this aspect of their identities.

After hearing the lively song "Twins," the children may have questions, such as what it's like to be a twin. There are many books available for children that deal with the topic of twins. For example, *Twins!*, by Elaine Scott, features a variety of identical and fraternal twins and is illustrated with color photographs. Check your library, bookstores, the Internet, and the reference list at the end of each activity to find books that are appropriate for your class.

TWINS

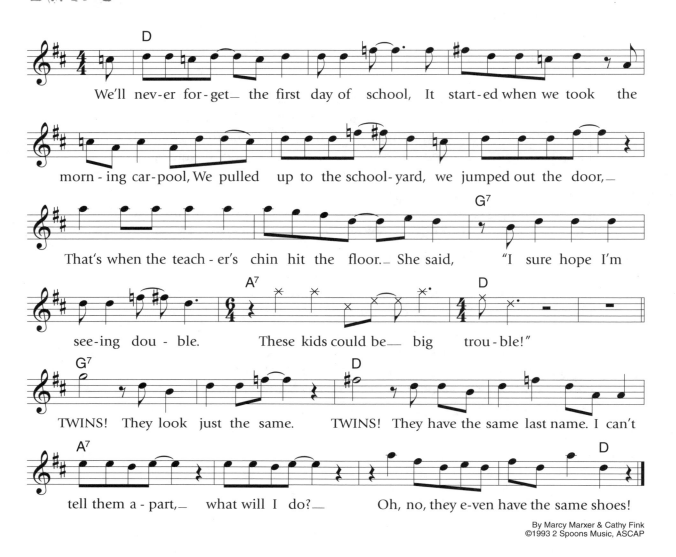

We'll nev-er for-get— the first day of school, It start-ed when we took the morn-ing car-pool, We pulled up to the school-yard, we jumped out the door,— That's when the teach-er's chin hit the floor.— She said, "I sure hope I'm see-ing dou-ble. These kids could be— big trou-ble!" TWINS! They look just the same. TWINS! They have the same last name. I can't tell them a-part,— what will I do?— Oh, no, they e-ven have the same shoes!

By Marcy Marxer & Cathy Fink
©1993 2 Spoons Music, ASCAP

Twins

by Marcy Marxer & Cathy Fink

(©1993 2 Spoons Music, ASCAP)

We'll never forget the first day of school,
It started when we took the morning car-
pool,
We pulled up to the schoolyard, we
jumped out the door,
That's when the teacher's chin hit the
floor.
She said, "I sure hope I'm seeing double.
These kids could be big trouble!"

chorus:
TWINS! They look just the same.
TWINS! They have the same last name.
I can't tell them apart, what will I do?
Oh, no, they even have the same shoes!

My sister and I knew just what to do,
We looked at each other, gave our secret
clue,
We put our knees together, we waved our
right hands,
And said, "Hello, Teacher!" in unison.
We marched to our seats, we turned on a
dime,
We sat down at just the same time!

chorus:
TWINS! We look just the same.
TWINS! We have the same last name.
She can't tell us apart, what will she do?
We've got the teacher completely confused!

The next day we wanted to trick the
teacher,
I wore sneakers, I wore patent leather,
I wore green, I wore blue,
It was really obvious who was who.
Then after lunch we traded clothes,
We knew the teacher would never know!

chorus:
TWINS! We look just the same.
TWINS! We've got the same last name.

We can be double trouble or twice
as funny.
We're drawn to fun like bears to
honey.

We walked into class, we traded seats,
We thought we were really neat,
The teacher called on me, I
answered in rhyme,
She called on me, I answered this
time.
She studied us hard, she took a few
notes,
She was a little smarter than we had
hoped!

The teacher looked at us, she started
to grin,
We knew our little game was about
to end,
She put her hands on her hips,
tapped her foot on the floor and
said,
"Hey, why didn't I see it before?
One has a freckle. One has a bigger
smile.
You can't fool me, I knew it all the
while!"

chorus:
TWINS! We thought we'd fool the
teacher.
TWINS! She was a clever creature.
Now the whole class knows how to
tell us apart.
How did our teacher get so smart?

chorus:
TWINS! Our birthdays are the same.
TWINS! We have the same last
name.
Sometimes we look alike and some-
times we don't.
But we're two different people and
that's no joke!

LEARNING ABOUT TWINS

Materials

group-time area, large enough for the children to sit comfortably
  together, or cozy reading area for reading to several children
  at a time
copy of *Twins!*, by Elaine Scott
additional books about twins
CD player

Directions

1. After listening to the song "Twins," read the book *Twins!* to the
   children. Be sure to hold the book so that the children can see
   the large, colorful photographs.

2. After reading each page, ask the children what seems the same and
   different about each of the children in the photograph.

3. Spaced throughout the book are questions for the children to think
   about, such as, "Is it hard for you to share your favorite toy?" Give
   the children time to think about and discuss these questions.

Discussion

The book *Twins!* points out that not all twins are identical, and
not all twins like to dress alike. Review these pages with the children and talk about them, using questions and comments such as
the following:

- Ask the children to think about their own families.
- If they have brothers or sisters, what's similar about them and their
  siblings? What's different?

Variations

1. Have other books about twins available in the classroom. The
   children can read them on subsequent days, or they can be shared
   during story or circle time.

2. Many more children have siblings than twins. There are many excellent children's books that deal with sibling issues. These should be included throughout the year in early childhood classrooms.

Children's Books

Bunting, Eve. *Twinnies*. San Diego: Harcourt, 1997. A young girl who has twin baby sisters expresses her feelings about being left out and superseded as daddy's special girl. She also finds that she adores her new sisters.

Hutchins, Pat. *Which Witch Is Which?* New York: Greenwillow Books, 1989. Two girls who are twins both dress as witches for a party. They each have their own likes and dislikes, however, and the children learn that because of this uniqueness, they can tell the girls apart.

Noll, Sally. *That Bothered Kate*. New York: Greenwillow Books, 1991. Kate's younger sister annoys her by copying everything she does. Then, when her sister makes friends of her own, Kate misses her. Mother reassures Kate throughout the book that this is all part of growing up.

Rotner, Shelley. *About Twins*. New York: Dorling Kindersley Publishing, 1999. This book clearly and simply answers many of the questions young children may have about twins. The large color photographs illustrate the concepts beautifully.

Scott, Elaine. *Twins!* New York: Atheneum Books for Young Readers, 1998. Described above.

Web sites

Twins magazine: www.twinsmagazine.com. Designed for parents of twins, this Web site recommends and sells books about twins.

Twinstuff.com: www.twinstore.com. This Web site has a section called "Twinstore" where books about twins are reviewed.

I'm Special in My Family

It's important to keep reminding children that twins are individuals. When they see two people who look alike, they must remember that each person is unique. Twins have their own likes, dislikes, feelings, and experiences. The children can better understand this idea by reflecting on their own families. What is similar about them and other family members? How are they different? The children can explore these ideas by looking at family photographs and writing their reflections.

Materials

family photograph for each child
white drawing paper
writing paper
colored markers or pencils

Directions

1. Send a letter home to the parents asking them to send a family photograph to class, or take a family photograph during a home visit.

2. Make color copies of the photographs.

3. Working in small groups, have the children glue the copy of their family's photograph to drawing paper and then draw their own version of their family next to it. Ask the children to compare how family members look and act as they work on their drawings.

4. After talking about their families, the children can write or dictate their reflections. The writing and artwork can be displayed together.

Discussion

Ask the children questions and make comments about their families that focus on similarities and differences. For example:

- Do you have the same color hair as anyone else in your family?
- Do you and your sister like the same toys or different ones?
- Does anyone ever get you mixed-up with your brother?
- What's really special about you in your family?

- Alejandro says that he and his brother both have black hair, but his is a little longer. His brother likes to play baseball, but he likes hockey better.

Variations

1. There are many excellent books about families. These should be available in the classroom while the children work on their family projects.

2. The children's artwork and stories can be assembled into a class book about families.

3. Children may wish to read their family stories and share their photographs and drawings during group time.

Children's Books

Bradman, Tony. *Daddy's Lullaby*. New York: Margaret K. McElderry Books, 2002. Daddy comforts baby until they both fall asleep.

Cowen-Fletcher, Jane. *It Takes a Village*. New York: Scholastic, 1993. In this West African village, everyone looks out for the children. This book broadens children's ideas about family and community.

Morris, Ann. *The Daddy Book*. Parsippany, New Jersey: Silver Press, 1996. With beautiful, oversized photographs, Morris shows daddies from around the world.

Morris, Ann. *The Mommy Book*. Parsippany, New Jersey: Silver Press, 1996. This complement to *The Daddy Book* shows mommies from around the world.

Animal Twins

The children may be interested to learn that many kinds of animals, including bears, deer, goats, and sheep, often have twins. Reading about animal twins and comparing their pictures is a way for the children to discuss similarities and differences. Some children may have had experiences with pets giving birth and may be able to relate how each kitten or puppy is a little different.

Children who know twins quickly learn that they are not really alike. Each has his or her own personality. The same is true in the animal world. Although many animals have two or more babies at a time, each baby is unique. Talking about animal babies, including how each is an individual, helps the children develop feelings of kindness and compassion.

Materials

selected books about animal babies, particularly those that discuss twin births

pictures of animal twins, available in books and on the Internet

Directions

1. Share examples of animal twins with the children at circle time, or with small groups throughout the day.
2. Ask the children to look carefully at the baby animals. Do they look exactly alike, or are they somewhat different?
3. Talk about what the animals are doing in the photographs. What seems to be different about how the animal babies are behaving?

Variations

1. Nothing can compare with real-life experiences for young children. A field trip to a pet store or petting zoo can help the children perceive the special nature of each animal. Children who have difficulty seeing the animals can feel them.
2. Another way to give the children firsthand experience with twin animals or littermates is to invite a visitor, such as a veterinarian,

to visit the class. Tell the visitor ahead of time that your class is interested in comparing animals from the same litter.

3. Videotapes of animals with twin offspring, such as bears, can show your class the differing personalities of twin animals.

4. Toy animals in the block or dramatic play areas allow the children to reenact animal family life.

Children's Books

Burton, Jane. *Baby Animals.* London: Crescent Books, 1978. This book, which includes excellent photographs, has a section on twins.

Buxton, Jane Heath. *Baby Bears and How They Grow.* Washington, D.C.: National Geographic Society, 1986. Bears often have twin cubs, as the children will learn from this informative book. It includes beautiful photographs.

Evert, Laura. *Whitetail Deer.* Minnetonka, Minnesota: NorthWord Press, 2000. The children can read about twin births in this book about deer.

Fleming, Denise. *Mama Cat Has Three Kittens.* New York: Henry Holt, 1998. Mama cat has three kittens, but one likes to go his own way. This delightful book reinforces the idea of uniqueness among littermates.

Pringle, Laurence. *Scholastic Encyclopedia of Animals.* New York: Scholastic, 2001. The children can look for animals that have twins or multiple births in this excellent reference book.

Windsor, Merrill. *Baby Farm Animals.* Washington, D.C.: National Geographic Society, 1984. The children can discover which farm animals give birth to twins in this outstanding book.

Fingerprints—All Unique

Each individual has his or her unique set of fingerprints. This activity allows the children to compare the fingerprint patterns of their hands with those of their friends.

Materials

several inkpads with washable ink
white paper
magnifying glasses

Directions

1. Working with small groups of children, help the children press their fingers onto the inkpad and then onto the white paper.
2. Repeat the process until each child has a clear set of fingerprints.
3. Wash hands.
4. Have the children return to the table to examine their prints with magnifying glasses. The children can compare the prints on each finger and then compare their fingerprints to those of other children.
5. At first, some children may have trouble distinguishing differences. Assist them in making initial comparisons by describing the patterns made by the lines on their fingers.

Discussion

Fingerprints are one noticeable way in which all of us are unique. Use questions such as the following to help the children think of other ways in which people differ. The children can compare the answers that are the same and different. Each day the teacher can ask for another response. Over time, each child will have his or her own unique profile.

- What's your favorite thing to do at school?
- What snack do you like the best? What snack do you not like?
- What song do you like the best to sing at circle time?

Variations

1. To make the fingerprints easier to see and compare, enlarge them on a photocopy machine. For children with visual disabilities, trace the major lines with puffy paint. The children can feel their prints after the paint has dried.

2. Copy the enlarged fingerprints onto overhead projector sheets. The children can lay the prints on top of one another to compare them. The fingerprints can also be projected onto the wall for the children to examine.

3. Ask a police officer to visit the class and explain how fingerprints can help solve crimes.

Children's Books

Bang, Molly. *Ten, Nine, Eight.* New York: Greenwillow Books, 1983. A father helps prepare his daughter for bed by counting down favorite items, including toes, in this charming book.

Ewald, Wendy. *The Best Part of Me.* Boston: Little, Brown & Company, 2002. In this delightful book, children of various ethnicities talk about their bodies. Each has a favorite part, from elbows to ankles. Photographs of the children illustrate their points.

A Kid Like Me

8

An important theme in the song "A Kid Like Me" is that children have choices about what their roles in life will be when they grow up, and that they can fulfill their dreams. Use this song to spearhead an ongoing project or unit on occupations in the community. After listening to the song with the children, list the jobs that the children are familiar with on chart paper, suggest some roles that they may not be familiar with, and then ask which occupations they would like to learn more about. The interests of the children will fuel the discoveries to come.

A Kid Like Me
by Cathy Fink & Marcy Marxer
(©1993 2 Spoons Music, ASCAP)

There once was a preacher, Martin Luther King
He worked day and night to hear freedom ring
From Selma to Montgomery he led the people
In a struggle to create equal rights for all people
He didn't use violence, no guns or knives
His message was one that revered our lives
We remember his speech, "I have a dream"
He did a lot for kids like you and me

refrain:
I live in a land where dreams come true
Where everyone says it can happen to you
Martin had a dream that he could see
And once upon a time he was a kid like me
Like me (like you)
Like you (like me)
Martin had a dream that he could see
And once upon a time he was a kid like me

An astronaut named Sally Ride
Known and respected nationwide
She was the first American woman in outer space
And she flew with the Challenger and took her place
In history! For the world to see
And now she's a heroine for kids like me

refrain:
I live in a land where dreams come true
Where everyone says it can happen to you
Sally had a dream that she could see
And once upon a time she was a kid like me
Like me (like you)
Like you (like me)
Sally had a dream that she could see
And once upon a time she was a kid like me

Now Mickey and Minnie and Donald the duck
Are cartoon characters all children love
Walt Disney created them for us to enjoy
He had a vision that included every girl and boy
And so did Dr. Seuss with the Cat in the Hat
We learned to read from his books, what do you think of that?

He had a dream that he could see
And once upon a time he was a kid like me

Like you (like me)
Like me (like you)
Dr. Seuss had a dream that he could see
And once upon a time he was a kid like me

There's Whoopi Goldberg, an actress and comedienne,
Amelia Earhart, first woman of the air
Thomas Edison invented the lightbulb
Zina Garrison, the tennis player

People you see every day of your life
Your teacher, bus driver, firefighter, engineer
Mechanic, doctor, computer programmer
Everyone plays an important part
And everyone's got some love in their heart
They may not be famous, but they all have dreams
And once they were kids like you and me

Like me (like you)
Like you (like me)
We all have dreams that we can see
Dreams of being what we want to be
So if you have a goal within your sight
It takes a dream to start your flight

It Can Happen to Us

Materials

chart paper, divided into three columns
CD player
books about various occupations

Directions

1. Listen to "A Kid Like Me" with the children, and then give each child an opportunity to talk about what they think they would like to be when they're older.

2. Ask the children to name some occupations they are familiar with, and list those in the left-hand column of the chart paper.

3. Add some occupations that you think the children might be interested in if they haven't been named already. Those can be listed in the center column.

4. Ask the children which occupations they would like to learn more about, and list those in the right-hand column.

5. Next, ask the children how they could learn more about those occupations. Ideas might include consulting books, doing online searches, talking with parents, taking field trips, and inviting classroom visitors.

Discussion

Sometimes when children start talking about occupations, stereotypical thinking emerges. For example, a child might say, "You can't be a police officer. You're a girl." This provides a good opportunity for discussion and can guide the teacher on how to progress with the project. One class invited a female police officer to visit, which countered the views of some of the children that women couldn't hold that role. Another class visited a ballet rehearsal so the children could see both male and female dancers.

Variations

1. There is a wide variety of books to supplement classroom libraries. Some ideas are listed below.

2. Field trips can be an important way for the children to discover various occupations; the trips don't have to be elaborate. One class took the city bus downtown and visited the workplaces of several parents from the class. Then they all had lunch together on the square.

3. A neighborhood walk may highlight a number of different occupations, depending on the location of your school. Even in suburban areas, the children may see gardeners, architects, mail carriers, construction workers, cable and phone line workers, delivery truck drivers, and others.

4. For children who are learning sign language, consult an American Sign Language book to learn the signs for various occupations. The whole class might enjoy learning these signs.

Children's Books

Aliki. *Digging Up Dinosaurs*. New York: Thomas Y. Crowell, 1981. Many children are interested in dinosaurs and paleontology. This book explains what paleontologists do. A videotape is also available.

Barton, Byron. *Bones, Bones, Dinosaur Bones*. New York: Thomas Y. Crowell, 1990. Written for very young children, this book also deals with paleontology. The text is short and repetitive.

Flodin, Mickey. *Signing for Kids*. New York: Perigee Books, 1991. This book has clear illustrations for many signs grouped by categories, such as food, animals, and sports. It is an excellent resource.

Kunhardt, Edith. *I'm Going to Be a Fire Fighter*. New York: Scholastic, 1989. In this story, a young girl is determined to become a firefighter like her father.

Matthias, Catherine. *I Can Be a Police Officer*. Chicago: Children's Press, 1984. This book is one of a series that discusses occupations. The books, which include color photographs, feature men and women from diverse ethnic backgrounds engaged in the various occupations. Other topics in the series are animal doctor, astronaut, auto mechanic, baseball player, chef, computer operator, doctor, firefighter, football player, model, musician, pilot, president, teacher, truck driver, TV camera operator, and zookeeper.

The Dream Wall

"A Kid Like Me" features children talking about what they would like to be when they're older. The song conveys the message that you first need to have a dream before you can fulfill it. This art-and-writing activity encourages the children to dream. As they envision what they would like to be as adults, they can express their ideas in both paint and words.

Materials

plain or lined paper, for writing
pencils
watercolor paper
watercolor paints
large piece of white paper, cut in a cloud shape

Directions

1. Introduce this activity after the children have had ample time to read about various occupations, talk about them, and incorporate them into their play.

2. Listen again to the recording of "A Kid Like Me."

3. Working in small groups, ask the children to think about their dreams for the future.

4. Assist the children in writing their ideas, or take dictation from the children who are too young to write themselves. (You may prefer to have all the children do their own writing, even if they are not yet at a stage of writing where they produce recognizable print.)

5. Mount the children's dreams to the large piece of cloud-shaped paper and hang it in the classroom or hallway.

6. At a later time, ask the children to paint their dreams for the future with watercolors. The paintings can be hung next to the stories on the dream wall.

Discussion

Some younger children will inevitably envision themselves in an impossible role in the future, such as a superhero. We can't (and shouldn't) take away children's dreams, but we can help them connect their dreams to reality. For example, if a child says she wants to be Spiderman, ask what it is about Spiderman that the child wants to be able to do. If the child says she wants to be able to climb tall buildings, comment that some people do indeed learn how to climb tall walls, and even mountains. If the child says that Spiderman helps people and catches bad guys, acknowledge that many men and women become police officers so they can help people.

Variations

1. Children's views of possible future occupations are limited by their exposure to people in these roles. Books can help expand their horizons. Include a variety of books about various people and occupations. The books should reflect people who are diverse in many ways, including age, race or ethnicity, gender, and ability.

2. Some children may wish to continue writing about what they would like to do in the future. Put supporting materials in the writing center, such as word cards with the names of various professions and small illustrations to help beginning readers. Include a fill-in strip for the children who are just beginning to write, such as

I want to be _____ when I grow up.

Children's Books

dePaola, Tomie. *The Art Lesson.* New York: Putnam, 1989. A young boy, who is already a devoted artist, holds on to his dream of developing his talents, even when it seems the school program may hold him back.

Krementz, Jill. *A Very Young Actress.* New York: Random House, 1991. With spectacular photography, this book describes the life of a young girl who portrays Annie in the musical. Other Krementz books include *Keshia: A Very Young TV Star, A Very Young Gardener, A Very Young Musician, A Very Young Skater, A Very Young Circus Flyer, A Very Young Gymnast, A Very Young Dancer, A Very Young Rider,* and *A Very Young Skier.*

Kunhardt, Edith. *I'm Going to Be a Police Officer.* New York: Scholastic, 1995. A young girl and her brother visit the police station where their father works. She wants to follow in his footsteps.

FINDING OUT ABOUT MARTIN LUTHER KING JR.

Prominent in the song "A Kid Like Me" are descriptions of some well-known people, including Martin Luther King Jr. Some children may know about him already, while others may not. Build on the references to Martin Luther King Jr. in the song by reading books about him to the children and inviting discussion.

Materials

group-time area, large enough for children to sit comfortably together, or small book-sharing area for smaller groups
one or more books about Martin Luther King Jr., such as *Happy Birthday, Martin Luther King*, by Jean Marzollo
CD player

Directions

1. Ask the children if they remember some of the people named in the song "A Kid Like Me." Replay the song if necessary.

2. Read a book about Martin Luther King Jr. to the children. *Happy Birthday, Martin Luther King*, by Jean Marzollo, has short, clear text and beautiful illustrations.

3. Lead the children in a discussion of the book. Ask questions to help them understand the material at a concrete level. For example:

- How would you feel if you couldn't eat in a restaurant just because of the color of your skin? Would that be fair?
- Imagine if you got on a bus with your friend, and the driver said you couldn't sit together because you didn't have the same color of skin. How would that make you feel?

4. Display the books about Martin Luther King Jr. in the book area where children can read them frequently.

Discussion

Prejudice and discrimination are not limited to black versus white. Teachers may have children in their classes whose parents recall signs that read, "No dogs or Indians allowed inside." Some children may have had names yelled at them or their families because of their ethnicity, race, or religious beliefs. While some children may be comfortable talking about these issues, others may not. What is important is to cultivate a communal feeling in the classroom where the children feel safe to express their feelings. That is why it is so important to have a curriculum that reflects each child's background. The children should be allowed to talk about their feelings and experiences when they are comfortable and never be put on the spot or forced to talk about things they would rather not share.

Variations

1. Some children have had few interactions with people of races or cultures other than their own. All children can benefit from books such as *The Other Side*, by Jacqueline Woodson. A winner of the Coretta Scott King Award, it explores the gradual coming together of two girls from different races whose world has been divided along racial lines.

2. Read multicultural books, including other books about Martin Luther King Jr., throughout the year. Don't limit the children's exposure to multicultural materials to one particular time of the year, such as Martin Luther King Day or Black History Month.

Children's Books

Marzollo, Jean. *Happy Birthday, Martin Luther King.* New York: Scholastic, 1993. This picture book discusses the life of Martin Luther King Jr. and the freedoms he fought for in language that young children can understand. Brian Pinkney's illustrations are beautiful.

Woodson, Jacqueline. *The Other Side.* New York: G. P. Putnam's Sons, 2001. An African American child wonders about the fence that separates the black side of town from the white. On the other side of the fence sits a white girl of the same age. Gradually the girls grow closer and closer to one another, until they sit on the fence together and eventually play. This moving book illustrates barriers that continue to separate us and the power of friendship to overcome them.

SALLY RIDE—THE WORLD OF OUTER SPACE

Sally Ride, the first female astronaut, is another figure described in the song "A Kid Like Me." In addition to being an astronaut, she has also written several books for children that deal with space exploration. Share books written by or about Sally Ride, or books that include female astronauts, with your class. Since many children don't envision women in the role of pilot or astronaut, these books help counter stereotypes about women's abilities and occupations.

Materials

one or more books about Sally Ride or astronauts, such as *Sally Ride: Shooting for the Stars* for primary-age children, or *I Want to Be an Astronaut* for younger children
copy of *To Space and Back*, by Sally Ride

Directions

1. Ask the children if they remember some of the people named in the song "A Kid Like Me." Replay the song if necessary.
2. Read the book you have selected about Sally Ride, or astronauts, to the class. In the case of chapter books, such as *Sally Ride: Shooting for the Stars*, you may decide to read one chapter a day. Ask the children to recall the steps she had to go through to become an astronaut.
3. Show the children Sally Ride's book *To Space and Back*. Read parts of it to older children or discuss the large, color, photographic illustrations with younger children.
4. Display the books about Sally Ride and space travel in the book area where the children can read them frequently.

Discussion

Use the following questions to counter the stereotypical beliefs that children often pick up from society that women can't hold certain roles.

- Did you realize before reading the books about Sally Ride that women are also astronauts?
- Can you think of any jobs that only men or only women can do?

Be sure to be accepting of the input the children give, even if it is inaccurate.

For example, if a child said that he didn't think that women could be firefighters, you might reply, "Hm. I wonder if you're right about that, Jason. I've heard some other people say the same thing, but I'm pretty sure I've seen women firefighters on television. How can we find out if there are any women firefighters?" This gives the children a role in seeking out answers while accepting their current level of knowledge.

Variations

1. As young children try to envision the roles that adults have in the world, they often try to process the information through play. Socio-dramatic play is a way for them to try out various roles in a safe environment. Support the children's interest in space travel by including space props in the dramatic play area. Large cardboard tubes covered in aluminum foil make acceptable oxygen tanks, and earphones from listening stations look like space communication devices. The children can attach gadgets, such as spools, buttons, and small boxes, to a large piece of cardboard to make a control panel for a spaceship.

2. Reading about Sally Ride may spark an interest in learning about astronomy for some children. Many excellent children's books are available. While preschool children may not yet be able to grasp the concepts, some are still quite interested in hearing about them. Older children can better understand what stars and planets really are.

Children's Books

Barton, Byron. *I Want to Be an Astronaut.* New York: Thomas Y. Crowell, 1988. For young children, this book is a perfect choice. It describes a space journey using very simple text and graphic illustrations. Both men and women astronauts are included.

Hurwitz, Jane, and Sue Hurwitz. *Sally Ride: Shooting for the Stars.* New York: Ballantine Books, 1989. This chapter book describes Sally Ride's training as an astronaut and flight on the space shuttle.

Rey, H. A. *The Stars: A New Way to See Them,* and *Find the Constellations.* New York: Mariner Books, 1976. These two classic books by the author of *Curious George* introduce children and adults to the night sky.

Ride, Sally. *To Space and Back.* New York: Lothrop, Lee & Shepard, 1986. This book describes a space journey, from blastoff to landing. Although the text is lengthy, you can use the large color illustrations to discuss the content of the book with younger children.

Rockwell, Anne. *Our Stars.* San Diego: Harcourt, 1999. Using simple language and clear illustrations, Rockwell describes stars, moons, and comets.

Sweeney, Joan. *Me and My Place in Space.* New York: Crown, 1998. This book, which features an easily understood text, discusses the solar system.

Wilson, Lynn. *What's Out There? A Book about Space.* New York: Grosset & Dunlap, 1993. This book, which contains more text, is a good match for many primary-age children.

May There Always Be Sunshine

9

"May There Always Be Sunshine" was made up by a little boy in Russia while splashing in the bathtub. His father heard him singing and wrote down the words. It passed from person to person throughout Russia and then (via folksinger Pete Seeger) to the rest of the world.

This soothing and restful song is perfect for transitions from active play to quieter activities, such as naptime or story time. You might play the song as a lullaby, to comfort and reassure the children as they fall asleep. The message from the song can also be woven into other parts of the day.

In addition to calming and reassuring the children, "May There Always Be Sunshine" provides second-language learning opportunities. The recording includes verses sung in Russian and Spanish as well as English, languages that may be spoken by some of the children in your program. Whether or not they speak Russian or Spanish, many children will notice that there are words on the recording they don't recognize. This is an opportunity for children in monolingual environments to realize that the same ideas can be conveyed in other languages. Some children may enjoy learning to sing the song in another language.

May There Always Be Sunshine

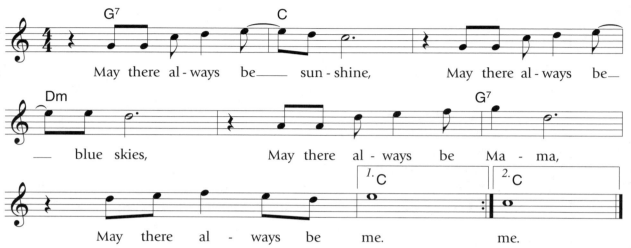

May there al - ways be___ sun - shine,   May there al - ways be___

___ blue skies,   May there al - ways be Ma - ma,

May there al - ways be me.   me.

Words: Russian—Lev Oshanin; English—Thomas Botting
Music: Arkadi Ostrovsky
©1964 by MCA Music Canada

May There Always Be Sunshine

Words: Russian—Lev Oshanin; English—Thomas Botting
Music: Arkadi Ostrovsky
(©1964 by MCA Music Canada)

English (2x)
May there always be sunshine,
May there always be blue skies,
May there always be Mama,
May there always be me.

Russian (2x)
Poost vsegda boodyet solntse,
Poost vsegda boodyet nyeba,
Poost vsegda boodyet mama,
Poost vsegda boodoo ya.

Spanish (2x)
Que siempre haya sol,
Que siempre haya cielo azul,
Que siemre haya mama,
Que siempre haya yo.

A Lullaby—Preparing for Quiet Time

Materials

CD player or tape recorder
copy of the song "May There Always Be Sunshine"
blank CD or cassette tape

Directions

1. Copy the song several times onto a blank CD or cassette tape.

2. As the lights are dimmed and the children snuggle beneath favorite blankets, play the recording to signal the transition to rest and slumber. Since the song has been recorded several times in succession, there will be several uninterrupted repetitions.

3. Staff who are comfortable singing can replace the recorded song with their own voices or quietly sing along with the recording.

Variations

1. Create a tape recording that includes the words to the song sung in the languages of the families in the program. The families or community members may be willing to assist.

2. Assemble a collection of lullabies that the children hear in their own homes and play those during rest time. If the children are second-language learners, some of the lullabies may be in their home languages.

3. Several recordings are available that include lullabies from around the world sung in the appropriate languages. Playing such lullabies reinforces the idea of similarities and differences: people all over the world sing to soothe their children, but their languages may be different.

Children's Books

Aliki. *Hush Little Baby.* New York: Simon & Schuster, 1968. Beautiful illustrations accompany the text of this Appalachian lullaby.

Bang, Molly. *Ten, Nine, Eight.* New York: Greenwillow Books, 1983. An African American father counts objects from ten down to one as he prepares his daughter for bed.

Brown, Margaret Wise. *Goodnight Moon*. New York: Harper & Row, 1947. In this classic, a young rabbit says goodnight to all the things in his room while his mother quietly knits.

Fox, Mem. *Time for Bed*. San Diego: Harcourt Brace, 1993. With beautiful pastel drawings and a lyrical, rhyming text, the author shows how animal mommies prepare their babies for sleep.

Wood, Audrey. *The Napping House*. San Diego: Harcourt Brace, 1984. In this hilarious, add-on book, a grandma is joined in her nap by her grandson and a host of animals.

Recordings

Epstein, Freyda. *Globalullabies*. Music for Little People, 42571. (www.mflp.com). Lullabies in English, Yiddish, Russian, Spanish, French, Czech, Japanese, German, and Nigerian.

Under the Green Corn Moon. Silver Wave Records, SC 916. This is a recording of Native American lullabies, sung in their original languages.

The World Sings Goodnight, 2 volumes. Silver Wave Records, SC 803, SC 909. Volume one includes lullabies from around the world, sung in thirty-three languages. Volume two adds thirty-two more lullabies.

BRIDGING CULTURES WITH SONG

Listening to soothing music sung in various languages helps children understand that all languages have ways to convey kindness and love. By translating the words to "May There Always Be Sunshine" into additional languages, you can convey the idea that mothers and fathers from around the world love and nurture their children. If possible, the languages selected should come from the families of the children in the program. This helps the children make the connection between languages and people of particular cultures.

Materials

sentence strips
poster board
marker

Directions

1. Speak informally to the parents or send a note home asking them to translate the words to "May There Always Be Sunshine" into their home language or another language in the community.

2. Transfer the words onto sentence strips and mount them on poster board. Some languages may be easier to write on the unlined side of the sentence strip.

3. Refer to the written words as the children sing the song in various languages.

Discussion

It is important for the children to be able to make connections between languages and the people who speak them. Be sure to talk with the children about each language and discuss who provided the words in that language. You may want to add a photograph of the family next to their translation of the song. Even better, ask if a member of the family would be willing to come to school and sing the song with the class. If they are uncomfortable singing, they can simply say the words in their home language.

Variations

1. Research on children who are bilingual or multilingual indicates that it is important for them to maintain their home language. Integrate first languages into the classroom by asking the parents to translate some of the children's favorite classroom books into their home language. The words can be written on sticky notes and mounted on the appropriate pages of the book. All children benefit from exposure to the rich diversity of languages.

2. Hearing their first language spoken is as important for second-language learners as seeing it in written form. Family members, family friends, or community representatives can tape-record the words to popular books in the home languages of the children in the class. In this way, they can hear the books in both English and their first language.

Children's Books

Ho, Minfong. *Hush!* New York: Orchard Books, 1996. A mother in Thailand scolds noisy animal visitors as she tries to get her child to sleep. The rhyming text and beautiful illustrations are very appealing to children.

Sardegna, Jill. *K Is for Kiss Good Night.* New York: Delacorte Press, 1994. This alphabet book, illustrated with oil paintings of multicultural children, uses bedtime phrases for each letter, such as "J—just one more story."

Scott, Ann Herbert. *On Mother's Lap.* New York: Scholastic, 1992. An Inuit mother rocks her child, along with an assortment of his toys, and lets him know that there is always room on Mother's lap.

Van Laan, Nancy. *Sleep, Sleep, Sleep.* Boston: Little, Brown & Company, 1995. Mothers from around the world sing their babies to sleep.

Adult Book

Moomaw, Sally. *More Than Singing.* St. Paul: Redleaf Press, 1997. This book includes songs and rhythmic activities with words translated into various languages. One activity is a lullaby, made into a big book.

OUR SPECIAL THINGS

"May There Always Be Sunshine" talks about four things that are very special: sunshine, blue skies, mother, and self. All of us have things that are important and special to us. This activity focuses the children's attention on things that are important to them, and then combines their individual ideas into a group creation.

Materials

group-time area, large enough for the children to sit comfortably together
mat or carpet square for each child to sit on
chart paper and marker
clear acetate overhead projector sheets
china markers (available in art and craft stores)

Directions

1. After singing "May There Always Be Sunshine" with the children, ask them to think about things that are special to them. List their ideas next to their names on chart paper.

2. Working in small groups, have the children use china markers to draw the things that are special to them on the overhead projector sheets. China markers adhere to the acetate and come in lovely colors.

3. Post the chart with the children's ideas near the work area so they can refer to it.

4. When everyone has finished, mount the artwork on the window to create a giant class quilt. The light will shine through the acetate and illuminate the drawings.

Discussion

Use questions and comments such as the following to help the children focus on the things that are special to them.

- Is there someone in your family who is extra special to you?
- Do you have something special that you always bring to child care with you? Is there something special you bring out at naptime?
- What kinds of special things do you do together with your family?

- Who are your special friends at school/child care?
- You and Jeremy both have dogs that are special to you. Jeremy's dog is named Jenny; your dog is named Prince.
- Vinh and Shelley both like to go to the May Day parade. That's a special thing they do with their families.

Variations

1. The children may also wish to write about their favorite things. Incorporate this into journal writing or introduce it as a special activity.

2 Encourage the families to send photos of friends or family members to school. The photos can be mounted on paper with photo corners, so that they are not damaged, and the names of the individuals can be included in the song. Write an individual verse for each child; for example:

> May there always be *Grandma*,
> May there always be *kitty cat*,
> May there always be *Will*,
> May there always be me.

Children's Books

Gomi, Taro. *My Friends*. San Francisco: Chronicle Books, 1990. With a simple, predictable text, the author recounts the many things we can learn from animal friends, such as "I learned to smell the flowers from my friend the rabbit."

Lionni, Leo. *Frederick*. New York: Pantheon Books, 1967. While the mice are busy preparing for winter, Frederick stores up remembrances of the summer and fall. Later, when it is cold and dreary, he puts these reflections into words to remind the mice of the wonderful things in life.

Porter-Gaylord, Laurel. *I Love My Daddy Because* . . . . New York: Dutton, 1991. Through illustrations of animal fathers, the author reminds of us of the special things about fathers, such as "he sings songs with me."

Porter-Gaylord, Laurel. *I Love My Mommy Because* . . . . New York: Dutton, 1991. In this complementary book to *I Love My Daddy Because* . . . , the special aspects of mothers are explored, such as "she goes swimming with me."

Rylant, Cynthia. *The Wonderful Happens*. New York: Simon & Schuster, 2000. This is a stunning book about some of the wonderful things in the world, such as fresh-baked bread, spiders spinning webs, and new-fallen snow.

SING IT IN SIGN

Yet another way in which many people communicate with one another is through American Sign Language. Individuals who are Deaf or severely hearing impaired, or who have a profound communication disorder, may use sign language. In fact, you may have children in your class or school who use sign. Children find it interesting to learn that they can communicate using their hands. Including sign language in activities such as singing raises their awareness of the many means that people use to communicate, as well as making those activities accessible for people who use sign.

Materials

illustrations of signs for key words in "May There Always Be Sunshine"
poster board and marker
group-time area, large enough for children to sit together comfortably
mat or carpet square for each child to sit on
CD player (optional)

Directions

1. Practice the hand signs for the following key words from the song:

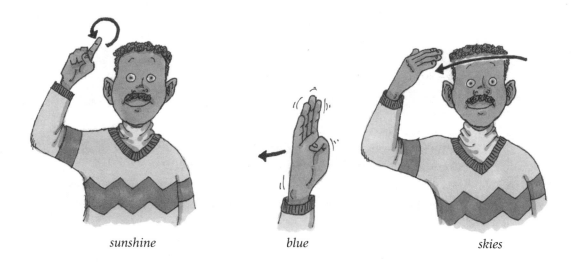

sunshine   blue   skies

mama

me

2. Copy the illustrations for the hand signals onto poster board.
3. Model signing while singing "May There Always Be Sunshine" with the children. If you are uncomfortable singing, use the recording as a backup.
4. Refer to the poster illustrations as an additional model. The children can refer to it throughout the day if they wish to sing the song.

Discussion

Unless there is a child or adult in the classroom who uses sign language to communicate, the children may view using sign language as just a fun activity. It's important to remind them that many people who cannot hear rely on sign language to communicate with other people. Learning sign language enables us to communicate with interesting people that we otherwise may not be able to "talk" to. Suggest to the children that as they get older, they may decide to learn more about sign language. Sharing books with the class about children who are Deaf and use sign language is a way to help them understand the meaning and purpose of American Sign Language.

Variations

1. Children gain a better understanding of concepts when they are used throughout the day rather than just during a prescribed activity. Try signing the words you have used in "May There Always Be Sunshine" at appropriate times during the day, such as when the sun comes out or Mama arrives for pick-up.

2. Build a sign language vocabulary with the children. Several children's books listed below give illustrations of signs for key words. Many children like to learn how to spell their name in sign language.

3. Having someone who communicates in American Sign Language visit the class helps children put sign language in an appropriate context. Children are amazed to see how quickly people who sign move their hands and the role facial expressions play in sign language. Contact Deaf advocacy organizations or your state's Center for Independent Living for resources.

Children's Books

Flodin, Mickey. *Signing for Kids.* New York: Perigee Books, 1991. This book has clear illustrations for many signs grouped by categories, such as food, animals, and sports. It is an excellent resource.

Litchfield, Ada B. *A Button in Her Ear.* Morton Grove, Illinois: Albert Whitman & Company, 1976. Angela, the young girl in this book, describes getting a hearing aid and why she needs it. This book helps young children better understand the challenges of people who are hard of hearing.

Peterson, Jeanne Whitehouse. *I Have a Sister: My Sister Is Deaf.* New York: HarperCollins, 1977. The children will gain a better idea of what it is like to be Deaf after listening to this story. Told by a child in first-person narrative, it emphasizes the abilities of her sister while not skirting the challenges.

Wheeler, Cindy. *Simple Signs.* New York: Viking, 1995. This book of simple signs is perfect for young children. The signs are linked with illustrations that show the derivation of the sign, such as a cat's whiskers for the sign for cat.

WALKIN' ON MY WHEELS

10

"Walkin' on My Wheels" is an upbeat song that emphasizes what people in wheelchairs can do. Thus, it builds on similarities. For example, the child singing the song talks about playing basketball, using a computer, and telling jokes—activities that most children enjoy. While some children may have friends or relatives who use wheelchairs, many have had little or no opportunity to know someone who uses a wheelchair. The song can be used as an introduction to stories that include children with wheelchairs, and help raise the children's awareness.

WALKIN' ON MY WHEELS

Swing tempo

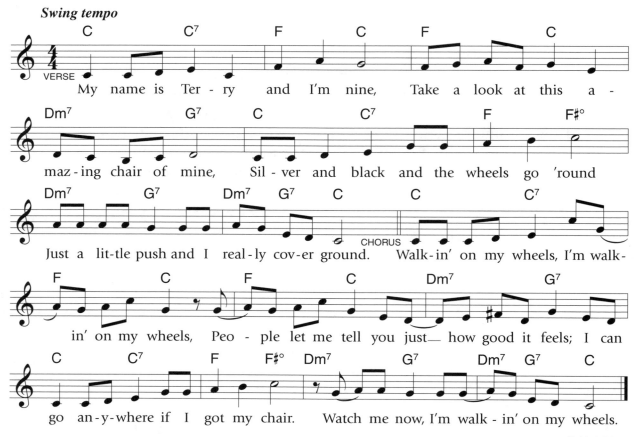

VERSE
My name is Ter-ry and I'm nine, Take a look at this a-
maz-ing chair of mine, Sil-ver and black and the wheels go 'round
Just a lit-tle push and I real-ly cov-er ground. Walk-in' on my wheels, I'm walkin' on my wheels, Peo-ple let me tell you just— how good it feels; I can
go an-y-where if I got my chair. Watch me now, I'm walk-in' on my wheels.

By Mark Cohen
©1986 Childsong Music, BMI

Walkin' on My Wheels

by Mark Cohen

(©1986 Childsong Music, BMI)

My name is Terry and I'm nine,
Take a look at this amazing chair
  of mine,
Silver and black and the wheels go 'round
Just a little push and I really cover
  ground.

chorus:
Walkin' on my wheels, I'm walkin' on
  my wheels,
People let me tell you just how good
  it feels;
I can go anywhere if I got my chair.
Watch me now, I'm walkin' on my
  wheels.

Why don't my legs work? I don't know,
Something happened to them very
  long ago,
But I work out every day and my arms
  are strong
They're just the thing for rollin' me along.

chorus

Every day when I go to school,
I ride in a van that's really pretty cool,
The lift takes my chair right down to
  the floor
Help me with the steps and I'll race you
  to the door.

chorus

Wasn't it funny when the substitute
  teacher,
Asked us to name that silly looking
  creature,
I raised my hand, she nearly dropped
  her chalk!
She thought I couldn't think just because
  I couldn't walk.

chorus

Can you come over? Ask your folks,
We can use the computer or just
  tell jokes,
And maybe later on I can come and
  visit you
If your building has a ramp, so my
  chair can visit too.

chorus

My friend Chuck has a chair like me,
But he's really old, he's almost 23,
He can shoot a basketball just
  like Dr. J
And just last week he started teach-
  ing me to play.

chorus

We All Use Wheels

This activity can remind the children of the many ways we all "walk on wheels." There is a big difference between using wheels for recreation and using wheels because it is the only way a person can move around. This activity builds on similarities—all of us use wheels for transport at one time or another.

Materials

group-time area, large enough for the children to sit comfortably together

strips of poster board or tagboard, 3 inches wide and about 20 inches long, to form the columns for the graph

small pictures of wheeled vehicles, cut from magazines or downloaded from Web sites

slips of construction paper, 2 inches long and ½-inch wide

marker

tape

Directions

1. Sing "Walkin' on My Wheels" with the children. Use the CD as a backup if you are uncomfortable singing.

2. Lead a discussion about wheelchairs using questions such as these:

- Have you ever known or seen someone who uses a wheelchair?
- Why do some people use wheelchairs?

3. Next, ask the children if they ever "walk on wheels," or use wheels to get around. List their ideas. They might include cars, scooters, bikes, skateboards, golf carts, wagons, and so on.

4. Tape pictures that match the children's ideas to the bottoms of strips of poster board. These will form the columns for a class graph.

5. If you don't have an illustration for an idea suggested by a child, quickly sketch it on the bottom of a poster board strip, or write the word for the object on the poster board.

6. Take each poster board strip, one at a time, and ask the children if they have ever ridden on that vehicle. Print the name of each child who responds affirmatively on a slip of construction paper and tape it to the poster board.

7. Continue the process for each vehicle. Once all of the columns are completed, tape them together to form a graph. Be sure to align the slips with the children's names on the columns. Drawing lines ½-inch wide ahead of time will help.

8. The activity can be extended over several days for younger children, who may lose attention if it is all done at one sitting.

Variations

1. The children may become very interested in various types of wheeled vehicles. Books about trains, trucks, and other vehicles with wheels can be added to the reading area.

2. The children may enjoy talking about wheeled vehicles as they add them to a flannelboard. Photographs such as those used for the graphing activity can be covered with Con-Tact Paper and laminated. Attach the hook side of a piece of Velcro to their backs and they will stick to a flannelboard. Be sure to include a wheelchair in the collection of photos.

3. Adding wheeled vehicles to the block area is a natural extension of interest in wheeled vehicles.

Children's Books

Barton, Byron. *Machines at Work.* New York: Crowell, 1987. For very young children, this book combines a simple text with clear, graphic illustrations.

Bingham, Caroline. *The Big Book of Things That Go.* New York: Dorling Kindersley Publishing, 1994. This is an excellent resource as the children explore things with wheels. The book is divided into sections, such as things that go on roads, in the city, on rails, and on farms.

Bingham, Caroline. *The Big Book of Trucks.* New York: Dorling Kindersley Publishing, 1999. Children who are fascinated with the many kinds of trucks will love this book.

Sturges, Philemon. *I Love Trucks.* New York: HarperCollins, 1999. Here's another book for the truck lovers in the class.

WILL MY LEGS STOP WORKING?

When young children first experience an individual with a disability, they are sometimes frightened. They may wonder if they can "catch it," or if exposure to the individual will cause a particular condition to "rub off" on them. Older children, or even adults, may wonder how to talk to the person, or if they should not look at the person because it may look as if they're staring. The best way to deal with these concerns is to talk about them openly. Books about children who use wheelchairs, coupled with sensitive discussions of the children's questions, can help alleviate their concerns.

Materials

group-time area, large enough for the children to sit comfortably together, or cozy reading area for reading to several children at a time

children's book that includes a prominent character in a wheelchair, such as *No Fair to Tigers*, by Eric Hoffman

Directions

1. Read the book you have selected to the children. *No Fair to Tigers* is especially interesting to children because of the story line. Mandy wants her toy tiger to be treated with respect, and "no fair" rings out throughout the book. The fact that the main character uses a wheelchair is not important until the end of the book, when she can't enter a store because of the stairs. Thus, the children get to know Mandy primarily as a person, not as a person with a disability.

2. Talk with the children about things that happen to them that they feel are not fair. Ask how they would feel if they couldn't go into a store or go to school because they needed a wheelchair and it wouldn't fit.

Discussion

A large question in many children's minds, but one that they may not express, is whether they can "catch" the disability through contact with the individual. Some children may even think that if they do something wrong, such as break a school or home rule, they could end up with a disability.

Adults can help the children by bringing these hidden concerns to the forefront and answering them respectfully and honestly. For example, say, "Sometimes children wonder why Mandy has to use a wheelchair. They may wonder if they can catch it, and if their legs will stop working too. Mandy was born with a condition that makes her leg muscles weak. That's why she uses a wheelchair. Mandy's friends can hug her and play with her as much as they like, and they can never catch what she has. It just doesn't work that way."

Mandy, the character in *No Fair to Tigers*, is adamant about not wanting to be helped too much. Treating people as less capable and able than they are is called "infantilizing," and it is often a problem for individuals with disabilities. After listening to and singing "Walkin' on My Wheels," ask the children what they think about the line that says, "She thought I couldn't think just because I couldn't walk." Don't be surprised if younger children agree with the comment. This is your opportunity to explain that having weak legs, or ears, or eyes has nothing to do with how well a person can think. Remind them of all the things the characters in the books you've been reading can do.

Children's Books

Brown, Tricia. *Someone Special, Just Like You.* New York: Henry Holt & Company, 1982. This book includes a child in a wheelchair, a child who uses a walker, and a child who uses sign language. With black and white photographs of children, it emphases the similarities among all children. Regardless of abilities or disabilities, all children like to do the same kinds of things.

Hoffman, Eric. *No Fair to Tigers.* St. Paul: Redleaf Press, 1999. This book shows Mandy, who uses a wheelchair, enjoying her day with her pet tiger. She likes to do the same things as other children, but is stymied by a store with steps. This brings home to children issues of wheelchair-accessible environments.

Rogers, Fred. *Let's Talk About It: Extraordinary Friends.* New York: Puffin Books, 2000. In his relaxed way of talking to children, Mr. Rogers discusses some of the key questions the children may have as they get to know children with disabilities. Six delightful children who have disabilities are featured.

What's It Like to Use a Wheelchair?

This activity addresses differences. It helps the children understand the reality of using a wheelchair in order to move. While wheelchairs enable individuals with physical disabilities to move around, buildings and streets pose many challenges. Much of our environment is not wheelchair accessible, a fact that people who are not dependent on wheelchairs seldom notice. This activity gives the children the opportunity to experience what it feels like to use a wheelchair, and also discover areas of the classroom or school that they cannot use while in the wheelchair. Wheelchairs can be rented from pharmacies or medical supply stores for a nominal amount of money: $15 per day or $25 per week is typical.

Please note: I would not recommend doing this activity in a classroom that includes a child who uses a wheelchair. The child might feel singled out and be uncomfortable with the activity. Children in a classroom that includes a child with a wheelchair are very fortunate because they will see firsthand the challenges posed by the environment and learn how to be a helpful and respectful playmate.

Materials

child-size wheelchair, available from pharmacies or medical supply stores
small notebooks or clipboards
pencils

Directions

1. Divide the children into pairs to use the wheelchair. They can take turns assisting each other. Post the list of pairs in the classroom and check off each pair as they take their turns. In this way, the children will know when their turn is approaching.
2. Establish safety rules with the children ahead of time and post them in the classroom. For example, the children should not run with the wheelchair or stand on it.
3. Give each child a notebook or clipboard. Encourage them to take notes on the things they can do in the classroom while in the wheelchair as well as the things they can't do. For example, does

the chair fit into the bathroom? Can they reach the easel to paint? Can they reach materials on the shelves? An adult can help the children with the writing if necessary.

4. When the children have all had a turn, gather them together and talk about their observations.

Discussion

Experiencing the use of a wheelchair firsthand helps the children understand the challenges posed by an environment that is not wheelchair accessible. Use questions such as these to help the children process their experiences with the wheelchair.

- What activities could you get to just fine using the wheelchair?
- What couldn't you do when you were using the wheelchair?
- What could we change in our classroom to make it work better for someone who uses a wheelchair?
- Think about something you did last weekend with your family. Do you think you could have done it if you used a wheelchair? Had anything been done to make the area or activity wheelchair accessible? What could be done so that everyone could have access to the building or activity?

Variations

1. If you have access to a wheelchair for more than one day, the children may wish to use it to explore other areas of their school. They can try out the wheelchair on the playground, in the lunchroom, or in the hallways (with school permission, of course).

2. Dolls with wheelchairs are available in early childhood catalogs. Adding such a doll to the classroom gives the children an opportunity to incorporate characters with physical disabilities into their play. This increases the awareness and comfort level of the children when they meet individuals in wheelchairs.

Children's Books

Cowen-Fletcher, Jane. *Mama Zooms*. New York: Scholastic, 1993. This book conveys a positive outlook by emphasizing all the things Mama can do in her wheelchair. As she cares for her son, the children see the similarities between a mother in a wheelchair and all mothers.

Fassler, Joan. *Howie Helps Himself*. Morton Grove, Illinois: Albert Whitman & Company, 1987. Howie is a child with severe cerebral palsy. This book documents his frustrations and triumphs as he finally, and laboriously, learns to move his wheelchair. It helps the children develop empathy and understanding for the difficulties people in wheelchairs may face.

Osofsky, Audrey. *My Buddy*. New York: Henry Holt and Company, 1992. The child in this book uses a wheelchair, but also has a helper dog. Children are fascinated to see all the things the dog does for his master, such as turning out the lights, fetching toys from high shelves, and carrying the money to the checkout in stores.

Turner, Deborah. *How Willy Got His Wheels*. Sun City, Arizona: Doral Publishing, 1998. The children will be amazed at this true story of a dog that uses a wheelchair.

Ramps and Bumps

The lyrics in "Walkin' on My Wheels" include the line "Help me with the steps, and I'll race you to the door" and "Maybe later on I can come and visit you if your building has a ramp so my chair can visit too." This points out the problems that people who use wheelchairs encounter when buildings are not wheelchair accessible. This activity allows the children to experiment with the problems that bumps and obstructions cause for wheeled vehicles, and possible solutions.

Children are acutely aware of issues of fairness. Their ideas about justice, and their ability to effect change, grow out of many small interactions in which they are encouraged to express their opinions and their ideas are accepted as valid. Involving the children in discussions of fairness in the community and listening to their suggestions teaches them feelings of empowerment. These are the individuals who will grow up to tackle problems in their communities and confront issues of bias and injustice.

Materials

small ramp, approximately 2 feet long and 1 foot wide, made from a hollow wooden-ramp block or a piece of wood or sturdy cardboard, elevated about 5 inches at one end

strips of wood molding, wide enough to go across the width of the ramp

small hooks or brackets, glued along the sides of the ramp, to hold the molding in place in various positions

small toy cars or vehicles, to roll down the ramp

Directions

1. Add the ramp to the science or manipulative area of the classroom. If you are making a ramp out of wood or cardboard, elevate one end by placing a block under it.

2. Start with one strip of molding. The children can move it to various locations along the ramp and observe what happens when the car hits the bump. Some children will turn the molding around so that the side with a gradual slope is facing the car. This creates a different reaction, and sometimes the car can roll over the bump.

3. Introduce molding of various heights for the children to try. They will notice that the higher the molding, the harder it is for the car to get over it.

4. Ask the children what they could do to help the car get over the bump. Some children may invent ramps made from paper or other art materials.

5. Take the children outside, a few at a time, to look at a curb or stair near the school. Ask them what they think could be done to help a wheelchair get over it.

Discussion

Ask questions and make comments such as the following to help the children assess the effect of their experiments:

- I see you put the slanted end of the molding on the uphill side. Did that make it easier for the car to get over the bump?
- Is the higher molding harder or easier for the car to get across?
- Do you remember when we were trying the wheelchair in our room last week? Did we find any bumps the wheelchair couldn't get over? Is this experiment with the molding giving you any ideas about how we could make it easier for the wheelchair wheels to roll over those bumps?

Variations

1. Take a walk with the children through the neighborhood that surrounds your school. Have the children look for "bumps," or places that would be hard for wheelchairs to maneuver over. Ask the children for suggestions to correct the problem, and write down their ideas.

2. Some children may wish to write to city officials, churches, businesses, or building owners to express concerns about the accessibility of their buildings. They can include some of their ideas for rectifying the problems in their letters.

Children's Books

Hoffman, Eric. *No Fair to Tigers*. St. Paul: Redleaf Press, 1999. The main character in this story can't enter a store because of the steps. The children may have some ideas for how to help after their experiments with ramps.

Osofsky, Audrey. *My Buddy*. New York: Henry Holt and Company, 1992. The child in this book uses a wheelchair, but also has a helper dog. Children are fascinated to see all the things the dog does for his master, such as turning out the lights, fetching toys from high shelves, and carrying the money to the checkout in stores.

Adult Book

Moomaw, Sally, and Brenda Hieronymus. *More Than Magnets*. St. Paul: Redleaf Press, 1997. Chapter 3 describes several ramp activities to incorporate into classrooms. Directions for making ramps are included.

Harry's Glasses

11

Many young children are familiar with people who wear eyeglasses. From the glasses that encircle mother's fond gaze to the teen in glasses serving ice cream at the mall, children realize that many people wear eyeglasses. What they often don't know is why. "Harry's Glasses," with its sometimes silly lyrics ("Then one morning he put his fork in his cereal") and more often serious text ("I can make some glasses that are just right for you") gives teachers and parents the opportunity to discuss with children the reasons why people wear glasses.

Harry's Glasses

Swing tempo

Har-ry was a hap-py kind of guy, He had curl-y red hair and
His moth-er said, "Har-ry, what's the matter?" But he ig-nored all of the

big green eyes. But one day he start-ed walk-ing in-to walls And the
chit-ter chat-ter. He could-n't read his name and the T V was blur-ry So he

kids picked him last____ when they were play-ing ball.
hugged his ted-dy who was soft and fur-ry.

REFRAIN
Har-ry had a problem, he could-n't see____ Eve-ry-thing as well as

you and me. He did-n't want an-y-bod-y to know So he

kept it a se-cret from head to toe.____

By Cathy Fink
©1993 2 Spoons Music, ASCAP

Harry's Glasses

by Cathy Fink

(©1993 2 Spoons Music, ASCAP)

Harry was a happy kind of guy,
He had curly red hair and big green eyes.
But one day he started walking into walls
And the kids picked him last when they
  were playing ball.

His mother said, "Harry, what's the
  matter?"
But he ignored all of the chitter chatter.
He couldn't read his name and the TV
  was blurry
So he hugged his teddy who was soft and
  furry.

Harry had a problem, he couldn't see
Everything as well as you and me.
He didn't want anybody to know
So he kept it a secret from head to toe.

Then one morning he put his fork in his
  cereal,
His mother said, "Harry, can this be real?
Your shirt is on backwards, your shoes are
  untied."
Harry looked scared and he heaved a sigh.

So that afternoon they went to see the
  optometrist,
And Harry sat in a great big chair for an
  eye test.
He looked at charts and balloons, numbers and letters
And wondered if the doctor could help
  make his eyes better.

Harry had a problem, he couldn't see
Everything as well as you and me.
It wasn't a secret anymore
And he waited for the doctor to tell him
  the score.

The doctor said, "Harry, I've got good
  news,

I can make some glasses that are
  just right for you.
Soon you'll be seeing with perfect
  vision."
A pair of new glasses was the doctor's decision.

So he danced with Harry into the
  hall,
With hundreds of glass frames on
  the wall.
Wire rimmed, plastic, purple, and
  green
More glasses than Harry and his
  mother had seen.

He tried on thirty different pairs of
  frames,
He looked in the mirror to see if he
  looked famous.
Or handsome or smart or silly or
  scary
He looked like a kid with glasses
  named Harry.

Then he thought of his teacher and
  he thought of his father,
They both wore glasses and they
  weren't bothered.
But he didn't want his teddy to feel
  left out
So he got a pair of glasses for the
  furry snout.

From that day on, Harry could see
Everything as well as you and me.
He still had to practice to get better
  at ball
But Harry had his glasses and—
  that's all.

WHY DO PEOPLE WEAR GLASSES?

Materials

group-time area, large enough for the children to sit together
  comfortably
CD player
copy of *Arthur's Eyes*, by Marc Brown

Directions

1. Listen to "Harry's Glasses" with the class. Encourage the children to sing along as they become familiar with the words.

2. Ask the children if they know anyone who wears glasses. After listening to their comments, ask them if they know why people wear glasses.

3. Next, read *Arthur's Eyes* to the class. The book explains why Arthur needs glasses.

Discussion

One of the issues that author Marc Brown explores in *Arthur's Eyes* is *ridicule*. Some people make fun of Arthur because of his mishaps when he's not wearing his glasses, and others call him names when he is wearing them. Use questions such as the following to explore this topic with the children:

- How do you think Arthur felt when people called him "four eyes" and laughed at him?
- Why do you think those people said those things to Arthur?
- What do you think Arthur could say or do to make himself feel better?
- Can you think of something to say to the people who teased Arthur to help them learn not to do that again?
- What if you were there at Arthur's school and you heard those other kids teasing him? What could you do to stand up for Arthur?
- If you were there, would you rather be the person who teased Arthur, or the one who stood up against the teasing?

Variations

1. Other books for children can help them understand visual disabilities. *Seeing Things My Way*, by Alden R. Carter, is a good choice. The illustrations show how things look to children who have various types of visual disabilities.

2. Many children receive vision screenings at school. Help prepare young children for this by including screening materials, such as eye charts and eye-cover paddles, in the dramatic play area.

Children's Books

Brown, Marc. *Arthur's Eyes*. Boston: Little, Brown & Company, 1979. Described on p. 132.

Carter, Alden R. *Seeing Things My Way*. Morton Grove, Illinois: Albert Whitman & Company, 1998. A young girl with a visual disability describes how things look to her. She also talks about other children in her school who have other types of vision problems, including some who wear glasses. The text and photographic illustrations are engaging and clear.

Through the Looking Glass

Lenses are curved pieces of glass or plastic that can enlarge objects (convex) or reduce them in size (concave). Convex lenses are thicker in the center than at the edges and are used in magnifying glasses. Concave lenses are thicker at the edges than at the center and are used to add clarity to images, such as in telescopes. Eyeglasses often have lenses that are a combination of convex and concave. They are carefully ground to suit each individual's eyes. This activity allows the children to explore the properties of lenses and thus better understand the function of eyeglasses.

The children may wonder about the purpose of a lens that makes things smaller. This is a good time to discuss the different ways that people see. Some people see things that are close to them really well, but things that are farther away are blurry. They are called *nearsighted*, and need concave lenses to correct their vision. Other people see clearly things that are far away but objects that are close to them, such as books, are blurry. They are called *farsighted* and need convex lenses to correct their vision. Different lenses, as well as lenses used in combination, are used to correct different problems.

Materials

magnifying glasses (both convex and concave are available in catalogs)
child's microscope
variety of objects with detail to view, such as seashells, rocks, woven fabric, and small pictures
observation notebook

Directions

1. Place the magnifiers and the objects in the science area of your classroom or group them on a tray in the manipulative area.

2. Ask the children to look at the objects carefully and then examine them again under the magnifying glasses.

3. Encourage them to look carefully at the lenses and compare the lens that magnifies with the lens that reduces objects in size.

4. After a few days of exploration, introduce the child's microscope. Some popular varieties are constructed so that both the top and bottom of an object can be viewed.

5. Have an observation notebook available so the children can record their discoveries.

Discussion

Use questions such as these to help the children observe carefully:

- Which lens helps you see the object more clearly?
- Does it make a difference how close you hold the lens to the object?
- What can you see with the lenses that you can't see without them?
- Does looking through the lens change how you see the colors of the object?

Variations

1. After the children have experimented with magnifying glasses and a simple microscope, add other types of viewing tools, such as binoculars or an inexpensive pair of "reading" glasses from a pharmacy. Ask for plastic lenses for safety.

2. The children can take the child-size microscopes outside to view objects in the natural world. One popular type of microscope allows the children to put objects inside and view both the top and the bottom of the item. With an adult's help, children can carefully put insects inside the microscope, view them from both the top and bottom, and then release them.

Children's Books

Brian, Sarah Jane. *Up Close! Exploring Nature with a Magnifying Glass.* Pleasantville, New York: Reader's Digest Children's Books, 2001. This book, which also includes a magnifying glass, features projects for exploring in the woods, in the water, on the beach, and in the backyard.

Wilsdon, Christina. *Far Out! Exploring Nature with Binoculars.* Pleasantville, New York: Reader's Digest Children's Books, 2000. This book comes with binoculars and includes projects for exploring in a city park, a pine forest, a stream, and others.

Web site

Marshall Brian's How Stuff Works: www.howstuffworks.com/lens. This Web site provides information about how lenses work so you can give clear and accurate answers to the children.

Finding Out Firsthand—Visiting an Optometrist

In the song "Harry's Glasses," Harry pays a visit to an optometrist. Optometrists are professionals who examine eyes and fit people for glasses. A visit to an optometrist can be fascinating for children. They can see the tools used to examine eyes and learn that eye examinations are not painful. The optometrist may give each child a chance to sit in the examining chair and look through several types of lenses. This gives them direct experiences with how lenses work. Later, if the children need to see an optometrist, they may feel much more comfortable because of this prior experience.

Materials

permission letter sent to parents
camera
book about eyeglasses, vision, or optometrists
poster board

Directions

1. After arranging for a visit with an optometrist, send a permission letter home to the parents describing the trip. You may be lucky enough to have a parent in your class who is an optometrist. Many adults wear glasses, so the parents in your classroom may have suggestions of an optometrist to contact.

2. Prepare the children for the visit by reading a book about children who wear glasses or talking about optometrists. Check the resource section below for ideas.

3. Talk to the children about what will happen on the trip. Remind them not to touch materials in the optometrist's office unless they are invited.

4. Write down an initial list of questions that the children have for the optometrist, and encourage them to ask questions during the visit.

5. Photograph each child trying out the lenses. If a child doesn't want to sit in the examination chair, take her picture in the office.

Discussion

Although the lyrics in "Harry's Glasses" say he walked into walls, it's important for the children to realize that most people who wear glasses can see well enough, even without their glasses, not to walk into objects or put their clothes on backward. Nevertheless, glasses are important because they enable people with vision problems to see clearly. As someone who wears glasses, I often have children ask me why I need them. I always explain that things look blurry to me without them, and the glasses allow me to see clearly. Since the children have trouble understanding what that means, whenever I show a filmstrip, I deliberately blur the image. "That's how I see without my glasses," I tell the children. Then I focus the image and add, "This is what my glasses do. They let me see clearly, like this." Firsthand experiences such as this really help the children understand why people need glasses and why they're important.

Variations

1. After the field trip, set up an optometrist office in the classroom. An eye chart and an eye patch, made from a cardboard disc attached to a tongue depressor, can be included.

2. Write a group thank-you letter to the optometrist. Each child can write or dictate what they especially liked or learned from the trip. This is a good way to express appreciation and also help the children recall their experiences.

3. Use the photographs taken on the field trip to document the experience. They can be glued to poster board along with comments from each child about the trip. The documentation panel can then be posted in the classroom for the children to read.

Children's Books

Adler, David A. *A Picture Book of Louis Braille.* New York: Holiday House, 1997. This book describes how Louis Braille, accidentally blinded as a child, grew up to invent the Braille alphabet.

Brown, Marc. *Arthur's Eyes.* Boston: Little, Brown & Company, 1979. Described on p. 132.

Carter, Alden R. *Seeing Things My Way.* Morton Grove, Illinois: Albert Whitman & Company, 1998. A young girl with a visual disability describes how things look to her. She also talks about other children in her school who have other types of vision problems, including some who wear glasses. The text and photographic illustrations are engaging and clear.

Kaleidoscopes and Prisms

Experimenting with kaleidoscopes and prisms is an exciting way to build on children's prior experiences with lenses. Kaleidoscopes are tubes with a combination of mirrors that create symmetrical images when objects are viewed through them. Some kaleidoscopes allow children to place small objects in the end of the tube and see how they look as they are rotated. Prisms are transparent objects, usually plastic or glass, with three flat sides and ends that are triangular. They break light into colors, so when children look through them, they see rainbows.

Materials

several kaleidoscopes, preferably with a removable bottom so the children can add objects to the tube
small objects to view through the kaleidoscope, such as pieces of ribbon, beads, or sequins
several small plastic prisms
observation notebook

Directions

1. Place several kaleidoscopes in the science or manipulative area of the classroom. The children can look at objects in the classroom and view the multiple, symmetrical images created by the kaleidoscopes.

2. Add the small objects to the area for viewing. The children can experiment by changing what is in the kaleidoscope and observing its effect on the image.

3. After several days, add the prisms to the area. The children can compare how objects look through the prisms to how they look through the kaleidoscopes.

Discussion

The children will naturally be interested in how kaleidoscopes work. Kits are available that allow the children to assemble and disassemble the kaleidoscope. After allowing older children to experiment with the kits, lead a discussion about what the children have discovered. For example, ask the children questions such as these:

- Did the kaleidoscope work when you took the mirrors out? Why not?
- What do you think the mirrors do?

Variations

1. Other interesting optical materials are also available. Inexpensive plastic cones or tubes, with glass bases cut in various patterns, are available in many toy stores. Since the tubes look the same until you examine the bases, the children are initially surprised to see that objects look very different when viewed through each tube.

2. Another interesting optical device is a periscope. Several sizes, from about 2 to 15 inches long, are available for classrooms.

3. Some kaleidoscopes made for children are specifically designed to allow them to draw designs and view them through the kaleidoscope. These make creative additions to a unit on optics.

4. Older children can make their own kaleidoscopes using paper-towel tubes and reflective poster board bent into a triangular shape.

A Book for All Ages

Boswell, Thom. *The Kaleidoscope Book: A Spectrum of Spectacular Scopes to Make.* New York: Sterling Publishing Co., 1992. This book is helpful for making kaleidoscopes. The children will enjoy viewing the beautiful kaleidoscopic images.

EVERYTHING POSSIBLE

12

In this sweet bedtime song, the singer talks about tucking a child into bed at the end of the day with visions of everything that's possible for that child in her life. Children are quick to pick up on limits that the culture around them may set on their dreams; this song is a powerful antidote to those limits. It discusses many possibilities for living one's life, and reassures the child that she will be loved no matter what choices she makes, and that the most important thing of all is the human connections she makes in her life.

Everything Possible

VERSE 1

We have cleared off the ta-ble, the left-o-vers saved, Washed the dish-es and put them a-way. I have told you a stor-y, and tucked you in tight At the end of your knock-a-bout day. As the moon sets its sail to car-ry you to sleep O-ver the mid-night sea, I will sing you a song no one sang— to me, May it keep you good com-pa-ny.

REFRAIN

You can be an-y-bod-y that you want to be, You can love whom-ev-er you will. You can trav-el an-y coun-try where your heart leads And know I will love— you still. You can live by your-self, You can gath-er friends a-round, You can choose one spe-cial one, And the on-ly mea-sure of your

By Fred Small

Everything Possible

by Fred Small

(©1993 Pine Barrens Music, BMI)

We have cleared off the table, the leftovers saved,
Washed the dishes and put them away.
I have told you a story, and tucked you in tight
At the end of your knockabout day.
As the moon sets its sail to carry you to sleep
Over the midnight sea,
I will sing you a song no one sang to me,
May it keep you good company.

refrain:
You can be anybody that you want to be,
You can love whomever you will.
You can travel any country where your heart leads
And know I will love you still.
You can live by yourself,
You can gather friends around,
You can choose one special one,
And the only measure of your words and your deeds
   will be the love you leave behind when you're gone.

There are girls who grow up strong and bold,
There are boys quiet and kind.
Some race on ahead, some follow behind,
Some go on their own way and time.
Some women love women,
Some men love men,
Some raise children, some never do.
You can dream all the day, never reaching the end
   of everything possible for you.

bridge:
Don't be rattled by names,
By taunts, by games,
But seek out spirits true.
If you give your friends the best part of yourself
They will give the same back to you.

refrain

Preparing for Dreamland

The first verse of "Everything Possible" talks about preparing for bedtime. Families have differing bedtime rituals. Some children may take a bath and read a story, while others may watch a favorite television show. This activity gives the children a chance to reflect on what the end of their day is like and compare it with their friends. It provides yet another opportunity for exploring similarities and differences.

Materials

parent letter
large sheet of pastel paper, cut from a roll
white construction paper
colored markers
yarn
CD player
tape recorder (optional)

Directions

1. Send a note home to the parents asking them to help their children remember which activities they do right before bed. Explain that this is part of a class reflection and writing project.
2. Working in small groups, play the first verse of "Everything Possible" several times and encourage the children to sing along.
3. Talk with each child about what activities they do before bedtime. Refer to the parent letters as you discuss each child's routine. Some children may want to record their responses on a tape recorder and listen to it later.
4. Assist the children in writing a list of their bedtime routines.
5. Encourage the children to use markers to illustrate their bedtime activities.
6. Cut a piece of white construction paper into a cloud shape, and write "Preparing for Dreamland" on it. Mount this label in the center of the large piece of pastel paper and attach both to a bulletin board or wall of the classroom.
7. Mount the children's lists of bedtime routines around the cloud shape and connect them to the cloud with pieces of yarn.

Discussion

During group time, sing the first verse of "Everything Possible" with the children, and then have them help you read their lists of bedtime routines. Use comments and questions such as the following to help the children see the similarities and differences between what they do at bedtime:

- Andy takes a bath at bedtime. Does anyone else take a bath at night? Oh, Kisu takes a bath too.
- Cecelia, does your mom or your dad read a story to you? Your dad? You know, I think Carmen's mom reads her a story. So you both listen to stories, but your dad reads yours, and Carmen's mom reads hers.
- Does anyone have a teddy bear they snuggle up with at night? Wow, look at all the children who have teddy bears: Ahmed, Lisa, Travis, Tyrone, Sage . . . . Does anyone take a different kind of stuffed animal to bed?

Variations

1. Some children may wish to write bedtime stories in small blank booklets. These can be prepared ahead of time by folding a piece of construction paper in half for the covers and stapling them together with half sheets of white paper for the interior pages.

2. There are many lovely children's books, representing various cultures and ethnicities, that focus on bedtime. These can be added to the book area and shared with the children.

3. Place a CD player in the dramatic play area of the classroom. Children may wish to sing along as they put doll babies or teddy bears to bed.

Children's Books

Field, Eugene. *Wynken, Blynken, and Nod.* New York: E. P. Dutton, 1982. This version of the classic children's poem, beautifully illustrated by Susan Jeffers, evokes the peace and tranquility of the bedtime world.

Morgan, Stacy Towle. *The Cuddlers.* Franklin Park, Illinois: La Leche League Intl., 1993. One by one, sleepy children wander down the hall until the whole family ends up cuddled together in the parents' bed.

Van Laan, Nancy. *Sleep, Sleep, Sleep.* Boston: Little, Brown & Company, 1995. Mothers from around the world sing their babies to sleep.

People to Know, Places to See

"Everything Possible" deals with separation and change in a positive way by emphasizing that the love family and friends have for one another never ends. Change is a constant in life, and it is helpful for the children to think about how positive change can be. This activity gives them an opportunity to share the special people and places they visit or have seen in individual books. The answers need not be exotic. A trip with Daddy to the corner market can be just as exciting and special to a young child as a long trip.

Some children become worried when they know a big change is coming. The birth of a baby, a move to another house, and entering kindergarten may make them feel anxious. After listening to the soothing recording and reading *Oh, the Places You'll Go!*, discuss changes with the children. During the spring, the conversation may focus on moving to the upcoming grade and what that will be like. Help children realize the many things that will stay the same. They'll still have their families, and they can visit their previous class and arrange to see their friends. Other things will be different and exciting because they're ready for new experiences.

Materials

CD player
copy of the book *Oh, the Places You'll Go!*, by Dr. Seuss
colored construction paper
inexpensive white paper, such as photocopy paper
fine-tip markers or colored pencils
binder or stapler

Directions

1. Listen to "Everything Possible" with the children. Ask them if there are any places they especially want to go.

2. Read *Oh, the Places You'll Go!* to the class or to a small group of children who are ready to work on their projects.

3. Preprint the words "People I Know, Places I See" on construction paper for the covers of the books.

4. Working with a small group of children, talk about some of the ideas from the book. Then ask the children individually what people and places they like to visit.

5. Help the children record their answers on the white paper. They can use one sheet for each person or place and illustrate them with fine-tip markers or colored pencils.

6. Continue the activity over several days or weeks. When the children are finished, assemble their pages into books using a binder or stapler.

Variations

1. Toward the end of the year, help the children cooperate on a class book called "The Places We've Gone, the People We've Seen." Children can draw and write about field trips the class has taken and special visitors. Photographs taken throughout the year can supplement the children's pages.

2. Help the children become more comfortable with change by sharing a variety of books with them that deal with changes in people's lives. Some notable examples are listed below.

3. If the children seem concerned about moving to the next grade, invite children from that grade to come and visit. They can tell the children what it's like in the "older" classroom.

Children's Books

Brandt, Amy. *When Katie Was Our Teacher.* St. Paul: Redleaf Press, 2000. This is a book of the reflections of children who are losing one of their teachers. They reminisce about all the great things she did with them.

Chestnut, Sheryl Daane. *I'll Be There.* New York: Simon & Schuster, 2002. Through lyrical text and lovely illustrations, a father reminds his child that he misses him during the day and thinks of him often.

Cohen, Miriam. *The New Teacher.* New York: Collier Books, 1972. When the classroom teacher leaves to have a baby, the children worry about what their new teacher will be like. They find that their fears are unfounded.

Keller, Holly. *Island Baby.* New York: Greenwillow Books, 1992. A young boy rescues a bird, and with the help of an elder, nurses it back to health. When it is time to release the bird, he has trouble separating from it. He asks his mother if she feels the same way about his leaving for school.

Seuss, Dr. *Oh, the Places You'll Go!* New York: Random House, 1990. Originally given as a graduation speech, this text speaks to people of all ages. A clear message is that things will not always go smoothly, but in the end, you'll succeed.

Udry, Janice May. *What Mary Jo Shared.* New York: Scholastic, 1966. A young girl eventually overcomes her shyness in kindergarten by sharing her father.

Special Memories—
Class Memory Books

Each year of school is a special time for children. As both parents and teachers realize, children change remarkably during a year's time. Class memory books, which include photographs of the children throughout the year, documentation of their activities, and samples of their work, are wonderful remembrances for the children and their parents. They also provide an excellent recording of the children's growth and development during the course of the year.

Materials

loose-leaf notebook for each child
photographs of the children throughout the year
paper
three-hole punch
clear page protectors, to hold artwork and work samples

Directions

1. Purchase a loose-leaf notebook for each child prior to the start of school. Notebooks are often less than $1 apiece during the back-to-school sales.

2. Throughout the year, take photographs of each child doing a variety of activities. Ask the parents to donate film.

3. Ask the children to select special artwork or work samples during the year to include in their end-of-year scrapbook. Photocopies can be made of work that is too special to leave at school but is also needed for the memory book.

4. Encourage the children to contribute special pages to the book, such as listing and drawing their friends, writing about their favorite activities, and listing their favorite lunch or snack foods.

5. As the end of the year approaches, punch holes in the pages and begin assembling the books.

6. Share the books with the children and their families on the last day of school. Both the parents and the children will be thrilled.

Discussion

"Everything Possible" addresses growing up, traveling, and separation. It also emphasizes that wherever you go, you'll always be loved and remembered. These can be difficult ideas for young children to understand. Use the following questions to discuss times when people have visited and then had to go away.

- Did anyone in your family have to leave for a while? Where did they go? How long were they gone?
- How can we show people we love them, even when they're far away?
- How do we help ourselves when we miss people we love?

Variations

1. Some pages for the memory books can be prepared ahead of time. This makes it easier at the end of the year. Examples might be a photograph of the school or the class photocopied for each child's book, pages about field trips, and name tags stapled to paper.

2. Young children may be a little hazy about how the postal system works. Have them draw pictures and write messages to send home. The children can mail them at a neighborhood mailbox or visit the post office. Then they can wait for the letters to arrive at their home.

Children's Books

Garland, Sherry. *The Lotus Seed.* New York: Harcourt Brace Jovanovich, 1993. A woman flees war-torn Vietnam, bringing only a lotus seed. She is heartbroken when the seed disappears, only to find a lotus tree growing in the backyard in the spring.

Isadora, Rachel. *At the Crossroads.* New York: Greenwillow Books, 1991. South African children eagerly await the return of their fathers, who have been gone for ten months working in the mines.

McCormick, Wendy. *Daddy, Will You Miss Me?* New York: Simon & Schuster, 1999. A young child, whose father has to be gone for a long time, learns to deal with his feelings and anticipate his father's return.

Waber, Bernard. *Ira Says Goodbye.* Boston: Houghton Mifflin, 1988. Ira feels sad and upset about moving and leaving his best friend behind, until his friend calls and invites him over to play.

Waddell, Martin. *Owl Babies.* Cambridge, Massachusetts: Candlewick Press, 1992. This book is already becoming a classic. Three baby owls are frightened when they awake to find mama gone. When she returns, she reassures them that she will always come back.

Keeping in Contact

As the end of the year approaches, many children worry about missing their friends and keeping in contact with them. This is the perfect time to introduce making address books. The children can record the addresses and phone numbers of their friends so they can write or call them during the summer months.

Materials

blank books, made by folding several pieces of paper together and stapling

index cards, each with the name, address, and phone number of a child in the class printed on it

pencils

CD player

Directions

1. Check with the parents ahead of time to make sure it is okay to share their addresses and phone numbers with the other families.
2. Print the name, address, and phone number of each child on an index card.
3. Working in small groups, assist the children as they copy names and addresses into their books. Extend the activity over several days if necessary.
4. The recording "Everything Possible" makes a soothing backdrop as the children work on their books.

Variations

1. Some children may wish to exchange e-mail addresses and contact each other using the computer.
2. If writing both names and addresses is too overwhelming for younger children, encourage them to write just the names and have an adult add the addresses and phone numbers.
3. Share books that show what kindergarten is like with preschool children who will be moving on to kindergarten. Knowing what to expect makes a new event less frightening.

Children's Books

Hutchins, Pat. *My Best Friend.* New York: Greenwillow Books, 1993. It seems that the "best friend" can do everything better, until a curtain blowing in the wind scares her. This book affirms the closeness of best buddies and the ways they help each other.

Keats, Ezra Jack. *A Letter to Amy.* New York: HarperCollins, 1968. One way friends can keep in touch is to plan a get-together and mail invitations. That's what happens in this book.

Lewis, Kim. *Emma's Lamb.* Cambridge, Massachusetts: Candlewick Press, 1991. Emma cares for a lamb that has lost its mother. When the mother sheep has been found, Emma has trouble letting go of the lamb. She discovers that the lamb belongs with its mommy, but will always love her too.

Udry, Janice May. *Let's Be Enemies.* New York. HarperCollins, 1961. Two boys, who are usually best friends, have a spat and decide they are now enemies. Soon they have made up and are sharing their skates and pretzels again.

Waber, Bernard. *Ira Sleeps Over.* Boston: Houghton Mifflin, 1972. Ira is excited about his first sleepover, but also a little scared. He finds out it's all right for his friend to know he sleeps with a teddy bear. His friend has one too!

Cathy Fink and Marcy Marxer

Cathy Fink and Marcy Marxer have delighted children, parents, and teachers with their interactive music for over 20 years.

Their experiences include classroom work, school assemblies, educational conferences, arts centers, and major concert venues. They have performed at the Kennedy Center, Philadelphia International Children's Festival, Smithsonian Institution, and on *The Today Show* and are frequently seen on The Learning Channel. They have presented keynotes, workshops, and concerts at conferences of the National Association for the Education of Young Children (national and regional), American Music Therapy Association, Southern California Kindergarten Conference, AFL-CIO, and hundreds of other organizations.

Empowering parents and educators to find more ways to include music in daily life with children has been a centerpiece of Cathy and Marcy's success. They are five-time Grammy nominees for the recordings "All Wound Up! A Family Music Party," "Pillow Full of Wishes," "Blanket Full of Dreams," "Changing Channels," and "Dreamosaurus." Other awards include The Parents' Choice Gold Award, The Oppenheim Toy Portfolio, American Library Association Award, Early Childhood News Award, and over 30 awards from the Washington Area Music Association.

Cathy and Marcy's live performances have set the standard for family participation and fun, and their recordings have inspired kids, parents, grandparents, teachers, and friends to sing together and enjoy the magic of music.

Children's and Family Recordings

Pocket Full of Stardust (Rounder, 2002)
All Wound Up/Cathy & Marcy & Brave Combo (Rounder, 2001)
Pillow Full of Wishes (Rounder, 2000)
Changing Channels (Rounder, 1998)
Blanket Full of Dreams (Rounder, 1996)
Air Guitar (High Windy, 1994)
Nobody Else Like Me (A&M, 1994; Rounder Records, 1998)
Help Yourself! (A&M, 1993; Rounder Records, 1998)
A Cathy & Marcy Collection for Kids (Rounder, 1994)
The Runaway Bunny/Goodnight Moon (with Si Kahn) (Harper Collins, 1989)
Kids Guitar 1 & 2 (Homespun Video, 1998)
Making and Playing Homemade Instruments (Homespun Video, 1989)
Ukulele Lessons for Kids (Homespun Video, 1993)
Cathy & Marcy's CD Songbook for Kids (Homespun Tapes, 1998)
When the Rain Comes Down (Rounder, 1987)
Jump Children (Rounder, 1986)
Grandma Slid Down the Mountain (Rounder, 1984)

Management/Bookings/Mailing List/Sales:

Community Music, Inc.
P. O. Box 5778
Takoma Park, MD 20913
800-669-3942
www.cathymarcy.com

Other Resources from Redleaf Press

Help Yourself! Activities to Promote Safety and Self-Esteem
by Kate Ross
Contains creative ways to use the songs from the CD *Help Yourself!* as a springboard into a curriculum for promoting self-esteem and safety skills among young children.

Changing Channels: Activities Promoting Media Smarts and Creative Problem Solving for Kids
by Eric Hoffman
Find positive ways to help children understand what they see on TV and in other forms of media. Each activity will help children learn important life skills while having fun.

More Than . . . Series
by Sally Moomaw and Brenda Hieronymus
This popular series is a child-centered integrated curriculum for five important areas of early learning: math, art, music, science, and reading and writing. Each book in the series offers answers to questions that teachers often ask and includes complete directions and illustrations for over 100 hands-on activities.

That's Not Fair! A Teacher's Guide to Activism with Young Children
by Ann Pelo and Fran Davidson
Real-life stories of children who worked together to address problems in their classrooms and communities, combined with their teachers' experiences and reflections, create a complete guide to supporting children's desire for fairness.

Big as Life: The Everyday Inclusive Curriculum, Volumes 1 & 2
by Stacey York
From the author of *Roots and Wings,* these two theme-based curriculum books offer sixteen information-packed units on favorite topics such as Family, Feelings, and Animals. Each has suggested materials, learning area set-ups, book lists, and loads of activities in all developmental areas. Every unit also includes ideas for field trips, classroom visitors, and activities to counter bias and stereotypes. An essential resource!

Lessons from Turtle Island: Native Curriculum in Early Childhood Classrooms
by Guy W. Jones and Sally Moomaw
Written by a Lakota man and a White woman, this is the first complete guide to exploring Native peoples with young children. Includes an introduction to Native issues in early childhood education as well as five cross-cultural themes with developmentally appropriate activities organized around children's literature—Children, Home, Families, Community, and the Environment.

800-423-8309
www.redleafpress.org